SAVOY HILL

the early years of British broadcasting

BRIAN HENNESSEY

IAN HENRY PUBLICATIONS

ISBN 0 86025 468 2

Printed by Redwood Books, Ltd.
Kennet House, Kennet Way, Trowbridge,. Wiltshire BA14 8RN
for
Ian Henry Publications, Ltd.,
20 Park Drive, Romford, Essex RM1 4LH

CONTENTS

ACKNOWLEDGEMENTS

The author would like to thank those who have kindly given permission for access to and the reproduction of photographs, plans, and written material, in particular:

Mrs. Leonore Symons, Archivist to the Institution of Electrical Engineers.

Mrs. Jacqueline Kavanagh, Head of the BBC Written Archives Centre.

Mr Roy Rodwell, Archivist to GEC - Marconi.

Mrs Symons and her assistant, Mrs Janet Smale, conducted me round the Institution building and adjoining Savoy Hill Mansions (now 'Savoy Hill House') on more than one occasion and allowed me access to all surviving plans of the building. While few of the plans showed details of the BBC occupation, they enabled the process of 'piecing together' to begin.

This process was made possible by three documents supplied by Mr Neil Somerville of the BBC Written Archives Centre, namely a staff list for 1926 with room numbers; a detailed summary of the space occupied by the BBC throughout the Savoy Hill years and two sketch layouts for 1923, showing how the rooms then in use were to be allocated. In addition, Mr Somerville let me see invoices relating to the conversion of space for studio and other uses.

Mr Rodwell drew my attention to a Marconi booklet of 1924 called *The Art and Technique of Broadcasting* which includes information on equipment in use at Savoy Hill. He provided photographs and other relevant material from the GEC-Marconi Archives. Most of the photographs are, however, from the BBC Photographic Library and Archive and I am grateful to Bobby Mitchell for her help.

I was able to check details of the BBC's occupation of the IEE Basement with Mr J. Herring who was employed in the Basement's Works Store in 1927.

BRIAN HENNESSY
February 1996

IEE Building, West Entrance at No. 2 Savoy Hill, April, 1923 *(reproduced by permission of Radio Press)*

INTRODUCTION

I. SAVOY HILL REMEMBERED

In Britain in the nineteen-forties, radio reached the height of its influence on the life of the nation and Broadcasting House provided its symbolic heart. At the start of that decade, no more than eight years separated Broadcasting House from its predecessor - Savoy Hill, yet the BBC's Savoy Hill days were already a fading memory and would soon become a mixture of legend and romance. For here it was that, in a spirit of improvisation, the BBC sowed its wild oats and grew into its full Corporate status.

The BBC occupation of Savoy Hill followed almost immediately after its birth at the end of 1922. The Savoy Hill era was to last nine years. But it was in the four pre-Corporation years, when BBC stood for 'British Broadcasting Company', that the greatest expansion and internal change occurred. By the end of its days the Company had taken up all the space that Savoy Hill could provide. The one building group between Strand and The Embankment housed all the Head Office functions along with the Engineering Department and the studios of 2LO, the BBC's London Station. Only technical considerations prevented the transmitter itself from being at Savoy Hill. It was located at Marconi House till 1925 when it was moved to Selfridges in Oxford Street, finally bowing out in 1929 in favour of the London Regional Station at Brookmans Park in Hertfordshire.

Richard Lambert, first editor of *The Listener*, writing at the beginning of the 'forties commented:

'To recall the petty details of life at Savoy Hill is no longer easy. Already memories of the Corporation's first home are growing dim in the minds of those who inhabit its giant successor, Broadcasting House. Yet the antiquarian of the future will surely scan eagerly whatever survives of its records, to try and piece together some account of that bustling, crowded, rather friendly and unpretentious place.' (Lambert, p.44)

But if the memories were growing dim just one decade later, we can only speculate as to whether they survive at all with the passing of a further half century. Hibberd himself, doyen of the Savoy Hill studios, writing at the beginning of the 'fifties already places the original studios on the wrong floors:

'There were then only two studios in use at Savoy Hill: No. 1 a large orchestral one on the ground floor, pleasantly decorated in blue and gold, and another general-purpose studio - No. 3 on the second floor.' (Hibberd, p.2)

In reality, the studios were on the first and third floors and it was the No. 3 studio which had blue and gold for its colour scheme.

But the Savoy Hill veterans, men like Hibberd, Grisewood, Gorham, Snagge, Maschwitz and Lambert, left some vivid accounts of life at Savoy Hill in the days when it buzzed as an exciting hive of broadcasting activity. Gorham and

Lambert recorded also the daily background life of the building with 'Joe on the lift and Bill on the door' - great characters. The lift at Savoy Hill was a small one and Joe, an ex-policeman, grew steadily larger until there was only room for a couple of passengers as well as him (Gorham p.24). Joe and Bill frequented Mooney's in the Strand as did Gorham himself. For his part, Lambert remembered the melancholy-looking man whose job was to hunt down mice; he remembered too the office-boys with wrists, hands and fingers soaked in black and scarlet ink for it was they who replenished the inkpots; also those 'officious little fellows' who would burst into the office with a weapon for flitting mosquitoes. 'A rain of fine mist, partaking partly of scent, partly of tear gas, would descend upon your head and shoulders provoking ignominious sneezes and imparting a slight irritation to the eyes and throat for the next ten minutes'. During the winter months as a precaution against flu 'stacks of paper cartons and bottles of Condy's fluid would make their appearance in the wash-rooms; and pontifical circulars directed staff how to gargle, when to gargle and what to gargle!' (Lambert, p. 45).

Yet, as Lambert had predicted, long after the Savoy Hill veterans had ceased to recall the great days, there would remain a desire, if only on the part of some 'antiquarian', to try and piece together an account of that 'unpretentious' place. The following pages attempt to do just this: to recreate Savoy Hill as it was in BBC days, floor by floor, room by room. We will then be better able to draw back the curtain on the BBC's formative years and to visualise the setting for those memories recorded by the wireless pioneers, memories of Savoy Hill as a 'bustling crowded and rather friendly place,' the hub of British broadcasting in the 'twenties.

But it was not a very friendly place when 75% of the BBC in the persons of John Reith, Arthur Burrows and Cecil Lewis first clapped eyes on it. Reith later recalled the occasion: it was the evening of Tuesday, 19 December 1922:

'We went to inspect sundry possible sites for the launching of our enterprise, each worse than the last. Finally, as dusk was falling, we came to Savoy Hill. It seemed the worst of all. What a depressing place it was. It had been used for some mysterious medical activities, vacated some months earlier and much dirt and depression had accumulated since then.' (Allighan, pp. 179/180)

The accommodation comprised an unused portion of the Institution of Electrical Engineers and, for reasons which will be given in Chapter III (Section 6), it was a remarkably sound choice. But it would be three months before the office staff could move in, and longer before the 2LO staff, with their needs for studio and amplifier accommodation, could take up occupation. In the meantime, the BBC was homeless.

But all was not lost. On 30 December, a few days after his first visit to Savoy Hill, the new Manager of the BBC, John Reith, made his way to Magnet

House, the Head Office of the General Electric Company in Kingsway, where he had been informed that temporary accommodation had been put at his disposal. A large notice in the GEC entrance hall announced: 'BRITISH BROADCASTING COMPANY - Second Floor'. On Monday, 1st January 1923, the BBC staff gathered together for their first working day - in one room!

Marconi's extended similar hospitality to the 2LO staff. In this instance three rooms were initially made available for exclusive BBC use - one for studio use, the others to house the transmitter and batteries. To operate the transmitter, which had been designed and constructed by Marconi staff, Marconi's lent their own engineers - again on a temporary basis. Marconi's had already provided nightly broadcasting since mid-November 1922 acting for the BBC pending the appointment of its first staff. Responsibility for the service lay with Arthur Burrows, himself a Marconi employee. The music side was directed by another employee - L. Stanton Jefferies. Jefferies continued in this role in the first weeks of the BBC era with Rex Palmer and a typist to assist him.

The temporary accommodation soon reached bursting point. Relief came in the nick of time with the Company's transfer to the building of the Institution of Electrical Engineers (IEE) in March 1923. The BBC occupied parts of the West and North Wings entered from No. 2 Savoy Hill. By mid-1924 all available space in the IEE building was packed to capacity. This time, relief came with the BBC's takeover of the large red-brick block which backed on to the north side of the IEE building - Savoy Hill Mansions.

But by the end of 1926 this too had become fully occupied. The two Savoy Hill blocks now housed nearly 400 staff and numbers were growing at 100 p.a.. This time there was no simple solution and the BBC simply erupted like a volcano scattering fragments of its departments month by month into any available space within half a mile of Savoy Hill. The scattered staff were not to meet again until May 1932, when the stately portals of Broadcasting House admitted them into its ordered interior.

From Savoy Hill programmes reached an ever increasing audience as more and more took out licences and distance became less and less of a problem. At first, the Marconi House 1½kW transmitter, linked to Savoy Hill, could serve the capital but little else. Early in 1925 its successor, the 3kW transmitter on the roof of Selfridges department store, Oxford Street, allowed Savoy Hill to be heard over most of Surrey and Hertfordshire, reaching out to Chatham and Maidstone in Kent and Maidenhead in the westerly direction. By that time Savoy Hill was also supplying the bulk of the programmes for a dozen major provincial cities by means of connecting Post Office land-ines. It was being heard in Sheffield, Liverpool, Leeds and Bradford, Hull, Nottingham, Stoke on Trent and even in Edinburgh and Dundee. Finally, in August 1925, a 25kW long-wave station opened at Daventry - Daventry 5XX. This station radiated 2LO programmes across rural

England reaching villages almost cut off from the mainstream of national life.

So, having spread its tentacles across urban and rural Britain, Savoy Hill became synonymous with 'broadcasting' in the mind of the British public. And all this within a brief four years.

2. SAVOY HILL RECORDED

The evolution of the BBC's occupation of Savoy Hill would be difficult to trace in any detail were it not for a useful digest prepared some years ago by the then BBC Archivist. Under the title *Savoy Hill: Summary*, this digest comprises a series of dated entries covering each stage of physical expansion and overspill during the period 1923 to 1932. Occasionally an entry describes not only the space taken, but the way it was used for studio, workshops, General Office etc. But the document rarely refers to the Department, or the Officer heading any Department which occupied the space referred to. Additional research has been needed to cover this side of the story.

Altogether, some 43 entries in the *Summary* relate to Savoy Hill in the period 1923 to 1932; 20 of these cover the Company years (1922 to 1926) and a further four complete the take-up of space. Fifteen entries describe the exodus, or at least, that part of it which spilled staff into nearby buildings. One entry shows that the search for a new permanent home commenced in the first 'Corporation' year - 1927. This search ended with the selection of the present site - Broadcasting House. The last three entries cover the move into Broadcasting House in 1931/32. Like Savoy Hill, Broadcasting House had to house both the London Station studios and control room and also all the Head Office functions. Like Savoy Hill, it was labyrinthine; and like Savoy Hill, it was not big enough to house every-body. But, in total contrast to Savoy Hill, it was purpose-built and conveyed a powerful image of the new medium as a dignified public service.

The layout of this book is largely based on the *Savoy Hill: Summary* and each Section of Chapters II, III, IV and VI relates to a particular entry or group of entries, these being set out at the beginning of the Section in question.

A Marconi House
B IEE Buildings
C Savoy Hill Mansions

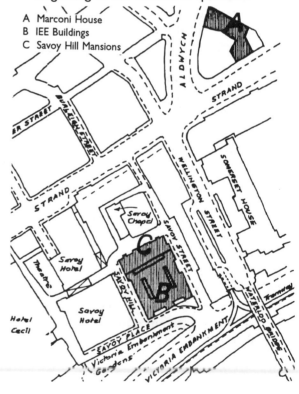

THE FLEDGLING B B C IN TEMPORARY ACCOMMODATION

I. MAGNET HOUSE, KINGSWAY (TEMPORARY HEAD OFFICE, BBC)

SH-SUMMARY: Entry - IA: 30.12.22. Head Office staff temporarily at Magnet House, Kingsway (General Electric Company's offices).

Magnet House opened in 1921 as the London Head Office of the General Electric Company. It was a magnificent modern office building which included retail and warehouse functions. It had a long sales counter at ground level with splendid showrooms below. The main offices were at first/second floors with stock rooms and packing facilities at upper levels. On the second floor were the Board Room, the top Management suite, Departmental Managers and General Office; the Accounts Department occupied the first floor (*Architects Journal*, 4 January 1922). In the circumstances, it is not surprising that at second floor level only one room could be allotted to the BBC. This room was about 30ft by 15ft being entered at one end, the door bearing the notice 'BBC: PLEASE WALK IN'. At the far end another door gave access to a tiny annexe six foot square. Both the room and its annexe had windows which looked into a light well close to the main lifts and stair.

Anyone who did walk in could take in at a glance the whole BBC staff - the Company Secretary (Anderson) and his assistant; the Director of Programmes and his Deputy (Burrows/Lewis); the Head of Publicity (Smith); the Chief, and only, Engineer (P. P. Eckersley); and 15 or so typists and clerks. A quiet corner in another room was soon found for the Accountant (Harley) and his assistant (Miss Mallinson). The General Manager, (John Reith) occupied the Annexe but his secretary (Miss Shields) used the main room. With six telephones on the go, type-writers clattering and press and public swarming in by open invitation, conditions were close to theatrical farce.

In the centre of the room stood a large table around which about ten people frantically sorted correspondence. The senior officials occupied different sides of the room with typists' desks, filing cabinets and duplicating machines stuck in every corner. There was no time for lunch; a cup of tea and a few sandwiches from the G.E.C. canteen would be swallowed at intervals between seeing countless people and replying to an infinite number of postal queries; for the office was bombarded not only by written requests for help but by people who, for some reason or other, were interested in broadcasting, arriving at all hours of the day. Apart from the press and the public, there was often a queue of manufacturers and retailers asking for information on BBC Membership, royalties, licences and technical matters. In the evening, boys from the Fleet Street newspapers would hang around the door waiting for the programme schedule for the next day to be completed and approved by Reith. In the end it became necessary to erect barriers between the visitors and the distracted staff.

The latter meanwhile increased in number almost daily until it became physically impossible to get any more in. Poor Burrows, carrying a heavy responsibility as BBC Director of Programmes, complained he had to place his hat on top of his walking-stick against a wall in order to find room for it! Burrows conceded 'We must have appeared as maniacs ... Throughout the day we worked like lunatics in a pandemonium such as I hope will never fall to anyone else's experience'. (Burrows, pp. 78/79: Lewis, pp. 26/28: Allighan, p. 167).

2. MARCONI HOUSE, STRAND (TEMPORARY LONDON STATION - 2LO)

SH-SUMMARY: Entry - 1B:30.12.22. London Station staff were already at Marconi House, Strand, where the studio and transmitter were situated.

Just as the General Electric Company offered the fledgling BBC temporary space in their Head Office, so also did the Marconi Company, space on the seventh floor of Marconi House being made available. For the Marconi Company this was not a new departure: over the previous months an experimental wireless station with the call-sign 2LO had been operating and developing. The coming of the BBC made little difference to the physical arrangements. Nor for that matter did its going: indeed the 2LO transmitter continued in BBC service long after the departure of the studio staff to Savoy Hill.

The original transmitter had been hurriedly put together in the early part of May 1922 in the laboratory of C. S. Franklin, one of Marconi's most senior and respected engineers. But in the autumn of 1922 a more powerful transmitter was constructed, this being gradually refined and developed over succeeding months. The four-panel 1½ kW transmitter that resulted became the prototype for the standard Marconi 'Q' transmitter soon to be installed in the BBC's provincial stations at Newcastle, Cardiff and Glasgow, and later at Bournemouth and Aberdeen.

On the roof immediately above the seventh floor Transmitter Room, the aerial likewise underwent development. In October 1922 it swept across open land linking Marconi House to Bush House; by the end of the year this had given way to two parallel aerials slung between the old masts on the east wing of Marconi House, each aerial consisting of sausage-shaped formations of wires.

By contrast programme development had been given rather lower priority in pre-BBC days. Much of the burden was initially carried by the Marconi Company's Publicity Officer, Arthur Burrows, in his spare time. Broadcasting as such was very limited in its scope. The first 2LO 'concert' (pianist, cellist and singer Charles Knowles) took place on 24 June 1922. At the beginning of August, L.

Marconi House, Strand, 1924 (*reproduced by permission of the Marconi Company, Ltd*)

Marconi House studio, 1922 *(reproduced by permission of Marconi's Wireless Telegraph Co., Ltd.)*

Stanton-Jefferies joined Burrows in a part-time capacity to help with the musical side of the programme. There was no budget to pay artistes who either gave their services gratis or were paid by outside organisations or individuals wishing to include broadcast appeals to aid Charities. Despite limitations in staffing and only nominal finance from Marconi's from 16 November 1922 a nightly 'BBC' programme was broadcast with news, talks, 'humorists', and 'concerts' the whole introduced by the 'chimes' of Big Ben played on a set of tubular bells.†

On the same floor as the transmitter, but overlooking the Strand, was a small cinema for showing trade films. It was to serve part-time as the studio for 2LO to the inconvenience of both parties. The room measured 23ft. 6in. by 18ft. 10in. but the slope of the Mansard roof reduced the effective width to about 15ft.

† On 21 January 1937 in a programme under the title 'Scrapbook for 1922', the BBC's first night was recreated with Leonard Hawke, the first BBC artiste, once again singing 'Drake goes West' on an old mic with piano accompaniment. A recording of the programme exists in the National Sound Archive.

It had a faded green carpet and, for acoustic reasons, its walls and ceiling were draped with two layers of thin white muslin which, in the sooty London air, soon became soiled and dingy (Lewis, p.29). In the earliest days it was referred to as the 'Concert Room' rather than the 'Studio' for, by the end of 1922, it was largely furnished for musical productions. A tiny orchestra of eight players occupied the centre facing the conductor's rostrum. Behind them and sideways on was a grand piano, the light from one of the two windows falling on the pianist's music score. The conductor had a direct view of the clock on the far wall below which was placed a set of tubular bells so that the evening's performance could start with a replica of the sound of the Westminster chimes and Big Ben. Against this wall too, was placed a desk for the use of the 2LO Director, Stanton Jefferies. His secretary's desk was placed against the opposite wall along with a gramophone and a 'divan' for waiting artistes.

Conditions in the room were not ideal for conducting auditions and rehearsals or preparing the evening concert. Lewis, writing a year later, recalled the two telephones 'which had a perfect mania for ringing; a typist who clicked away cheerfully morning, noon and night; engineers tapping, whispering and shouting into the microphones insisting on silence while they did so; artistes arriving fifty per day and crowding into the one room - the Studio - to await their turn for audition. 'Amid all this Mr Jefferies, single-handed,

attended to everyone producing at the end of the day a three hour musical programme' (Lewis, pp.29/30).

The news bulletins were prepared by Reuters and phoned through to Marconi House where they were taken down by a stenographer and typed. They were then phoned through to each of the other BBC stations - Birmingham, Manchester, Newcastle and, from March 1923, Cardiff and Glasgow. A room next to the studio was provided for this purpose as from 23 December (Letter from Burrows to Reith, 8 May 1937, in the BBC Archives).

Having designed the transmitter to his liking in 1922, H. J. Round, Marconi's leading British engineer, turned his attention in 1923 to the microphone. Within a few weeks, if not days, he developed the 'electrodynamic' microphone, a massive 20 lb cylinder resting on a bed of straw (later of rubber) laid on top of a used wooden valve box, itself placed on a sort of piano trolley (Stanton Jefferies writing in *Popular Wireless*, 5 October 1935).

The new microphone however needed a powerful amplifier. This amplifier was so large and so temperamental that it had to have a room of its own. It was duly constructed in the cinema's projection room where it was approached in silence and on tip-toe, its football-size valves glowing with a blinding brilliance. Unfortunately, there are no pictures of the amplifier even though this survived in use well into 1924. Nor has the author seen any photograph of the electrodynamic microphone in its earliest form mounted precariously on a 'soapbox'.

With the establishment of the BBC in meaningful terms at the very beginning of 1923, Stanton Jefferies was made full-time Director of 2LO, the London Station, with Rex Palmer as his Assistant Director. Other staff included Miss H Esmond (News Stenographer) and Miss Cecil Dixon (Piano Accompanist). Miss Dixon, as 'Aunt Sophie', joined Jefferies (Uncle Jeff) and Palmer (Uncle Rex) every evening at 5 p.m. to present the Children's Hour. They were joined in the studio by Burrows (Uncle Arthur) and Lewis (Uncle Caractacus) who would arrive breathless from Magnet House. Soon more staff were appointed; Lilian Taylor became the 2LO Secretary and Frank Hook its Music Purchaser/Librarian.

The cinema-studio was wholly devoted (though on a temporary basis only) to broadcasting and the London Station was allocated Room 107 as its official address, the phone number being CITY 8710 (CITY 8715 for the studio).

Years later, when there was talk of reconstructing the first London Station as a museum piece, Burrows and Jefferies drew plans and sketched the 'Soapbox' microphone. Jefferies recalled the shelf over the kitchen range which served for the BBC's Music Library (Letters from Burrows/Jefferies to Reith, May 1937, in BBC Archives). Petersen, the Marconi engineer in charge of the transmitter, also recalled the layout - and even the room numbers. 'The original and only position (of the transmitter) was Room 102 with Room 115 as our Battery Room.

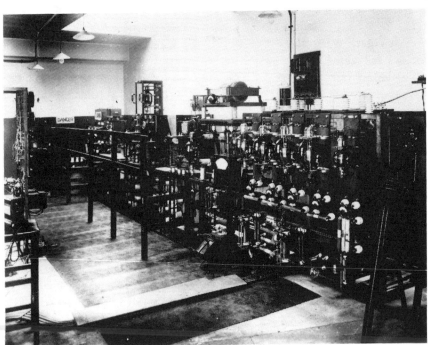

The first 2LO transmitter, 1923
(reproduced by permission of The Marconi Company, Ltd)

SAVOY HILL

I. HEAD OFFICE STAFF MOVE TO SAVOY HILL

SH-SUMMARY: Entry - 2:19.3.23. Magnet House staff moved to Savoy Hill. Offices rented on second and third* floors of the northern and western wings. Option taken on further empty offices in block.

'Savoy Hill' at this stage comprised space for renting within the building of the Institution of Electrical Engineers and in particular, its West Wing. This was approached from the building's West

Entrance at No. 2 Savoy Hill. The building is mainly of brick and has ground, first and second floors rising about 60ft and a top floor, originally concealed from view behind an elaborate cornice. The top floor had roof lighting. The building has four sides or 'wings', its hollow core containing at ground and first floor levels the Institution's lecture hall. The premises were designed by Stephen Salter and opened for medical use in 1889. Institution occupation began in 1909, but much of the space within the wings was made available for letting to 'allied' companies or organisations with electrical interests. The BBC was an obvious

The Institution of Electrical Engineers, 1923 *(reproduced by permission of the IEE)*

candidate as it was, in 1923, largely financed by major electrical companies intent on selling wireless receivers.

The leasing arrangements are discussed in more detail in Section 6, but the initial lease covered seven rooms on the second floor in the West and North Wings and one on the third (Appleyard, p. 257). Plans in the IEE Archives help us to identify the rooms in question. The West Wing contained at each level just two rooms these being separated from each other by a stone stairway entered from No. 2 Savoy Hill. The rooms were large, the North Room being 44ft by 26ft and the South Room 60ft by 21ft. They were also high at 18ft. The North Wing by contrast was more readily available for office use each level being 11ft high and divided by brick walls into five south-facing offices looking on to the interior of the block. These offices had angled fireplaces and a linking corridor. The North and West Wings were joined by the North West Stair where lavatory accommodation existed. The entry at No. 2 included a lift operated by IEE staff during working hours.

It was to the second floor rooms, suitably sub-divided, that the 31 BBC staff and their General Manager moved from Magnet House on Monday, 19 March 1923 (Briggs - II, p,465). The BBC had a home of its own.

In the BBC Archives there is a sketch plan by Reith showing the arrangements as at July 1923 and, with one exception, these applied to the original (March) allocation:

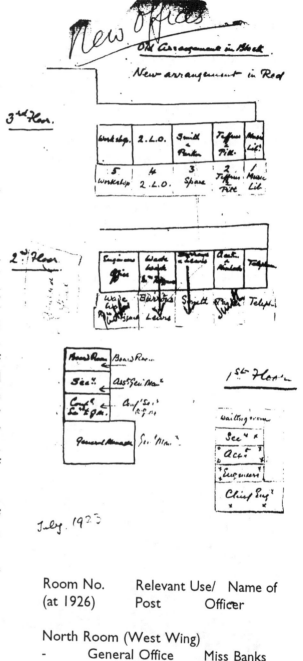

Room No. (at 1926)	Relevant Use/ Post	Name of Officer
North Room (West Wing)		
-	General Office	Miss Banks
-	Registrar	Page

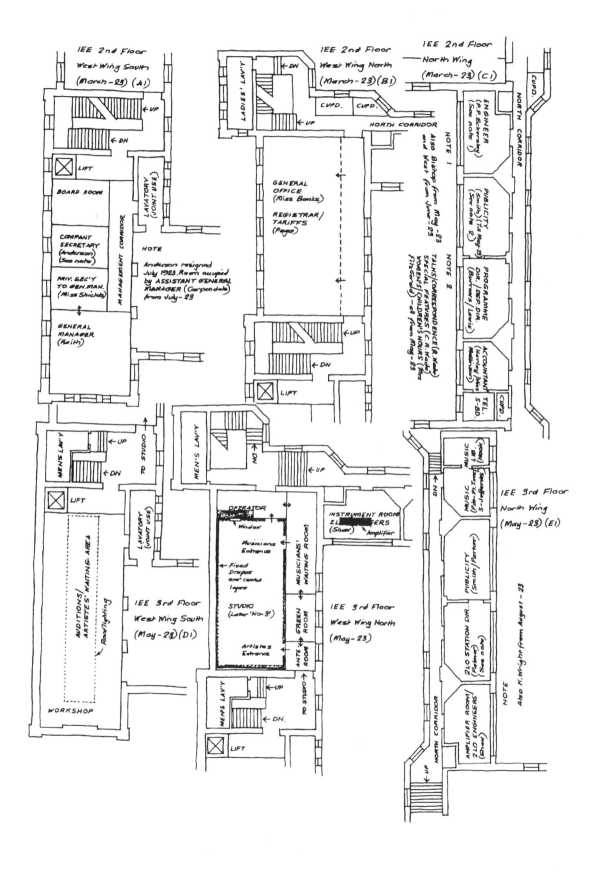

South Room (West Wing) (from South)

7	General Manager	Reith
8	Priv. Sec'y. to GM	Miss Shields
9	Company Secretary	Anderson
10	Board Room	

North Wing (from West)

16	Chief Engineer	Eckersley
17	(see below)	(see below)
18	Programmes	Burrows/Lewis
19	Accountant	Harley/Miss Mallinson
20	Telephone s-b	Miss May

Some of the original invoices for construction, lighting and furnishing survive in the BBC archives and they show the original use of Room - 17 as being for the Publicity Officer (Smith). But, more importantly, they show how the North Room on the third floor was prepared for studio use in the period mid-March to end-April.*

The South Room had what were termed the 'best offices' Reith's domain. They were approached through a glazed swing door and had their own lavatory. The offices were thickly carpeted, papered and equipped with coat rails. Pendant bowl lamps were supplemented by bronze standard lamps with green and white opal reflectors. Pictures completed the decor and the Company Secretary's office was fitted out with a safe.

The General Office occupied the North Room. It had glazed spring doors at each end of the adjoining corridor. An old table was renovated and covered in baize. On the floor was lino. Two rows of plain pendant lamps with 'Aladdin' shades served for lighting. A hat/coat rail was supplied and a stand with a zinc tray put in the corridor for umbrellas and wet clothing. A cupboard nearby had a kettle for making tea. The lavatory adjoining was altered for ladies' use.

In the North Wing, the four offices for senior staff were improved. The old stoves were re-enamelled and carpets, pictures and opal bowl lamps provided a touch of luxury for the Chief Engineer and heads of programmes and Publicity. In the Telephone Room a reflector light was fitted over the switchboard.

All windows were made to work smoothly and equipped with sprung Holland blinds.

The BBC was now housed in accommodation of dignified character and in a pleasing and central location. At its door a newly appointed Commissionaire (Plater) took up his position on Monday, 19 March to guide visitors, artistes - and indeed staff! It was Plater who pinned the BBC's name-plate in position on the right of the entrance at No. 2. It was his own handiwork and bore the words: 'BRITISH WIRELESS BROADCASTING CO. 2nd Floor', the name being suitably embellished with electric flashes. When the brass nameplate finally arrived some months later, Plater was loathe to remove his handiwork but was, in the end, prevailed upon by Reith to do so.

* The layout of the Studio suite is described in the next Section and details of the Studio's construction are given in Chapter V (Section 1).

2. 2LO STAFF MOVE TO SAVOY HILL/ FIRST STUDIO OPENED

SH-SUMMARY: Entries - 3, 4 and 5: April/May 1923. Marconi House staff moved over to Savoy Hill, ie London Station: Studio first used: Studio officially opened by Lord Gainford. (Later known as No. 3 Studio).

On 25 March 1923 a new lease was agreed to include additional space on the third floor. As with the second floor, the BBC took the two big rooms in the West Wing and the five rooms comprising the North Wing. This allowed for the 2LO staff transferring from Marconi House and also for the studio and associated accommodation, the Marconi House studio being taken out of service. As the transmitter at Marconi House continued in use, a linking land line had to be provided between the two buildings.

Apart from the Marconi House staff (chiefly Stanton Jefferies and Rex Palmer, who ran the 2LO Station, and Shaw, the studio engineer responsible), accommodation had to be found for new specialised sections responsible for talks, special features, Women's and Children's Hours and Music. The Archive sketch plan referred to in the previous section shows how this was arranged:

Room No. (at 1926)	Relevant Use/ Post	Name of Officer

North Wing, Third Floor (from West)

24	2LO Workshop	Shaw
25	2LO Director	Palmer
26	Publicity	Smith/Parker
27	Music	Pitt/Jefferies
27A	Music Library*	Hook

North Wing, Second Floor (from West)

16	Engineers	Eckersley/Bishop
17	Talks/Correspondence	R. Wade
17	Special Features	C. R. Wade
17	Women's Hour/ Children's Hour	Mrs Fitzgerald

The North and South Rooms on the third floor contrasted with those in use by the BBC on the second floor in that they were almost wholly dependant on roof lighting, having blank walls, exposed roof trusses and a clear internal height of only 11 ft. But these characteristics made them very convenient for studio and workshop use as sound could be excluded and the walls draped or made available for fixing instruments and other equipment.

It was in the North Room that the new studio suite was built. The specification notes of the contractor, Wallis & Sons, are dated March 1923 (amended 5 April) and show what was involved.

The North Room, measuring 44ft by 26ft, was divided by two new walls to create a studio 37ft by 18ft. The narrow space at the end (north end) became the 'Operators Room', whilst that at the side of the studio was made available for a waiting or 'green' room, an ante-room and Musicians Waiting Area. The idea seems to have been for artistes to enter the studio and leave via the ante-room. The 'Green Room' and 'Ante Room' had windows looking into the interior of the IEE building.

The studio structure was completed by sealing off the roof space with joists and boarding. The walls and ceiling were then lined with five layers of canvas at inch intervals and finished with decorative saffron-yellow gathered netting, the aim being to reduce reverberation to a minimum. The microphone could thus respond accurately to the voice impinging on it, as if it were in the open air.

Like the studio, the microphone was entirely new and still in the experimental stage. Known as the 'magnetophone' it was cylindrical and lay on a cushion of sorbo-rubber which held it in a sling supported in a wooden frame. The frame was initially covered in material and looked like a small meat-safe. In the first few months the 'meat-safe' was perched precariously on the old tripod that had carried the electrodynamic microphone at Marconi House. Eventually it was given a purpose-made four-legged stand.

As with the electrodynamic microphone, the magnetophone needed a very powerful amplifier in its immediate vicinity. Accordingly the Marconi House amplifier was transferred to Savoy Hill and located close to the studio. Given that it was 8ft long, 2ft deep and nearly

* In May 1923 it contained 500 items (Goatman, pp. 62/63)

5ft high, it was far too bulky to fit into the Operator's Room. The only obvious alternative was to put it, together with its batteries, in the Workshop in the North Wing adjacent to the studio suite.

A contemporary description paints a 'science fiction' picture: 'Silent men wearing headphones stand before a multitude of switches, dials and glowing bulbs' to 'control blasting and the degree of amplification before the currents conveying the reproduced effects pass via a cable to Marconi House where the transmitting apparatus (is) situated.' (E. Alexander writing in *Broadcast Listeners' Year Book 1924*).

Appropriately, the Operators' Room has been termed the 'Listening Room'. The engineer in this room listened in to the performance to check its quality as received. He was able to advise the announcer as to where the artiste should stand in relation to the microphone. He did this by signalling through a sound-proof window. He also controlled the studio lights and fans and was in touch by phone with the engineers controlling the transmitter in Marconi House.

The studio was dark, oppressive, stuffy and acoustically dead but the BBC

(reproduced by permission of Hulton Deutsch Collection, Ltd.)

The BBC Wireless Orchestra, conducted by Stanford Robinson at Studio December, 1923

19

Layout of Studio suite, May, 1923 *(reproduced by permission of the Illustrated London News Picture Library)*

was at some pains to overcome its essential dreariness. To contrast with the saffron-yellow walls and ceiling, blue was added to the colour scheme in the form not only of the thick carpet but by introducing blue pilasters on the walls. The circular tables were also painted blue and the settees and armchairs were covered in blue and gold striped linen. Even the 'meatsafe' microphone box was covered in blue and gold, only the exposed front being screened with black net material. It was almost too much. The initial dozen unpolished chairs were soon replaced by black, waxed polished chairs which must have afforded a welcome contrast. A small conductor's platform was provided. Lighting was by two bowl lamps suspended on oxidised silver chains; two-lamp silver brackets with shades were fitted to the pilasters. A half length pilaster was added as an after-thought to the southern wall to carry the studio clock. Ventilation was provided by ceiling louvres hiding air shafts fitted with exhaust fans. These were, however, too noisy to be used whilst broadcasting was in progress.

The Waiting Room was approached from the Ante-Room through a door set in a glazed wooden partition. Here again were blue walls, and blue and gold striped linen on the settee and the seats of the mahogany chairs. A mahogany writing table and a wall mirror were thoughtfully provided, along with a stand for hats and coats. A notice requested Artistes 'Not to talk loudly'. The floor was carpeted in grey haircord and artificial illumination was by Italian alabaster bowl lamps.

Beyond the Artistes' Waiting Room was the more basic Musicians' Waiting Lobby or 'Band Room', with access to the Studio via the north door. Here the Wireless Orchestra assembled, the space being equipped with a dozen chairs along with two Windsor armchairs and a window seat. An upright piano and a couple of tables completed the furnishings, the floor being covered in cocoa-fibre matting. The little room was sometimes used for auditions.*

Later, in 1924, when the Studio became for a while a specialised one for talks and drama, the Band Room functioned as a property area and resembled 'an old-time marine store', for it contained the implements for producing dramatic sound effects such as rotating cylinders gripped by bands of canvas, shallow drums, metal sheets, hollow pipes with chains etc. (Burrows, pp. 98/100).

With only limited space, the Waiting or 'Green' Room was essentially for the next item on the programme (E. Alexander, op. cit.). Others had to wait in the big South Room beyond the entrance stair. With its undecorated walls and exposed metal roof trusses, this was a gloomy room and one where peace was liable to be shattered by auditions taking place and by engineers attending to equipment at the far end. Reith was troubled at the thought of artistes having

* In May 1923 an average of 250 artistes a week were given auditions at Savoy Hill or up to 72 in a single day (Popular Wireless, 26 May 1923: this issue includes a photograph of auditions in progress in the Musicians' Waiting Room).

to 'use the room where the workshop is situated and where auditions take place' (Letter to Binyon, 20 July 1923 in BBC Archives) and this may have been the occasion for his instruction to engineers not to 'show their braces whilst working if there are visitors around'.

(reproduced by permission of the Marconi Company, Ltd.)

Artistes' reception room, late 1923

3.   SPACE ON FIRST FLOOR TAKEN/ ARTISTES RECEPTION ROOM

SH-SUMMARY: Entry - 6: Summer 1923. Large room on first floor taken and divided into five rooms. (Later known as Engineering Corridor.)

Reference was made in the previous Section to the lease of 25 March 1923. This included not only the space described above but also the 'room on the south west corner of the first floor' *i.e.* the South Room. The BBC was however in such financial straits that the room was not taken despite severe over-crowding.* By July congestion reached desperate proportions. At the same time the BBC's financial prospects were looking more rosy with the Postmaster-General's Sykes Committee actively devising a new basis for the BBC's finances, less dependent on the sale of receivers by BBC member companies. Reith accordingly prepared the case for completing the plan drawn up in March by taking the first floor space and by sub-dividing the South Room on the third floor to provide a good quality Reception Room.

* The rent was accordingly reduced from £2050 p.a. to £1600 p.a., a saving of £450 p.a.

In making his case Reith pointed out that the Company Secretary (Anderson) had lost his accommodation to the new Assistant General Manager (Carpendale); that the Engineers' Room was overcrowded with five people (probably West Eckersley, Bishop, and two secretaries); that Page, the Company Registrar, had to work in the General Office 'amid the continual roar of typewriters'; that the Music Section - Pitt, Jefferies and their assistant - were squeezed into one room; and that the Accountant and his two assistants also had to make do with one small room. 'We propose', he wrote, 'to divide the large room which is underneath my office (i.e. the South Room, first floor) into five separate offices'. (Letter dated 20 July from Reith to Binyon, one of the BBC directors, in the BBC archives). With his letter Reith enclosed a sketch plan showing how the existing accommodation would be reorganised.

The first floor was to be allocated:

Room No. (at 1926)	Relevant Use/ Post	Name of Officer
South Room, First Floor (from South)		
1	Chief Engineer	Eckersley
1	Dir. Eng. Research	West
3	Dir. Eng. Maintenance	Bishop
3	P.A. to Ch. Engineer	Carter
3	Eng. Development	Pitt
4	Accountant	Harley
4	Cashier	Miss Mallinson
5	Company Secretary	R i c e (replacing Anderson)
6	Waiting Room	

The effect would be to release Rooms 16 and 19 in the North Wing, second floor, which could thereupon be re-allocated to Parker and Smith respectively, reflecting Parker's new role as BBC Editor of the *Radio Times*, the first issue appearing in September 1923.

All this is shown in Reith's sketch plan of July 1923, his second thoughts being shown in blue over the red pencilled proposals. But Reith did not foresee the impact of the SB equipment then being installed at the end of the South Room on the third floor. From September this would allow the six (soon to be eight) BBC Stations to share selected programmes with each other, a process known as 'networking'. Somebody had to act as a central co-ordinator and this task fell to Lewis, who was given the title 'Organiser of Programmes'. Gerald Beadle was appointed in September 1923 to help with this work and all the hectic activity and phoning it involved. Lewis and Beadle needed a room of their own and Mrs Fitzgerald and her assistant, Miss Thomas, who looked after Women's and Children's Hours were moved to Parker's Room.

Meanwhile a large board was fixed to the wall of Room - 17. This was divided into days with hours along the top and the stations listed down one side all ready for the 'game' to commence. Lewis described this 'game' three months later in his book:

'It is a sort of glorified "happy families" where everyone is asking everyone else what they have got or what they want. "Can you give me the Savoy Orpheans at nine forty-five? Thank you very much. Good-bye". A big chart hangs on (my) office wall which shows what everybody is supposed to be doing for two months ahead. As events are offered to stations, their acceptance is (shown) on the chart'

As if solving this 'maddening jig-saw' were not enough, Beadle also had the job of compiling the programme pages of the Radio Times using the big 'chart' for this purpose. This meant weekly visits to Fleet Street with the constant fear of last minute alterations requiring revisions to the proofs. Thus the inception in September of both networking and the *Radio Times* led to much frantic action and 'tearing of hair' in Room - 17 (Lewis, pp. 66/67). At all events, Burrows and his secretary, Miss Huntington, were left in peace in Room - 18, having an office to himself as befitted his seniority as Director of Programmes.

All these changes depended on the BBC securing the first floor accommodation. In this, Reith was not disappointed. Reith's proposal was agreed and a new lease was drawn up on 22 August 1923 very much reflecting the earlier lease of 25 March. The space was formally occupied on 7 September the new higher rental being payable from that day. Page it seems continued to work 'amid the roar of typewriters'. The over-crowded Music Department, however, used the now vacated Room 26. This room adjoined the Station Director's office on one side and the Director of Music's room on the other and into it

moved Wright, soon to be followed by the Music Department's Secretary (Dorothy Wood) and a month or two later, Stanford Robinson. (Kenyon, p.6).

The second part of Reith's plans concerned the long South Room on the third floor. He had been conscious of the fact that there was 'nowhere for the better class of artiste to wait and no proper workshop for the Development Section'. Accordingly he proposed 'to divide up the room into Waiting Room, Audition Room and Workshop'. Surviving invoices show that of the five bays two were reserved for the Reception Room, two for Auditions and one for the Development Section.

In the event, the Reception Room and its approach from the lift were, by Savoy Hill standards, relatively luxurious. All was 'good taste, neatness and peace' (E. Alexander, *op. cit.*). A new ceiling was provided incorporating a large lantern light, the whole designed to mask the roof trusses and existing lantern light. The ceiling was 'panelled out' and edged with a cornice. The walls were likewise panelled out and distempered and stippled to special instructions. The floor was covered in a best quality grey Axminster carpet and settees and arm-chairs similar to those in the studio were provided, only covered in grey. The dark mahogany chairs had matching grey cloth seats and a circular mahogany table was in the centre of the room, with small square tables near the walls. A piano was provided for any artiste wishing to rehearse, and a receiver with a large horn allowed those in the room to listen to the performance from the nearby studio (Eckersley referred to the Reception Room as the 'Listening-in Room').

A communicating door led from the Reception Room to the Auditions Room. This too had a ceiling but was altogether more sparingly furnished. A plain brown lino covered the floor and, in place of settees and armchairs, a long wall seat and twelve black waxed polished chairs were provided together with a circular deal table.

The end bay served as a workshop for the Development Section and was equipped with work bench and shelving. But it was a room which no visitor to Savoy Hill would wish to miss, for here was housed the S. B. Board. 'Simultaneous Broadcasting' (S.B.) meant that a broadcast from Savoy Hill could be relayed by cable to any other BBC station and radiated simultaneously in the area served by that station. In short a speaker in London could be heard in cities throughout Britain if the BBC so wished. From 29 August 1923, the newsreader in the Savoy Hill studio was heard nightly throughout the land: gone were the days when the news had to be phoned through to each of the five provincial stations (Burrows, p. 91). And this new miracle of wireless depended on a rank of Western Electric amplifiers fixed to a board about six foot long and railed off from the remainder of the workshop.

At this time, the arrangements for general circulation were simple in the extreme. Everybody used the one entrance at No. 2 Savoy Hill where the white card announcing the BBC's presence had been replaced by a smart brass name-plate. A few outside steps led up between railings to the door beyond which lay a small bleak hall with a stone stair leading upward. A sign however pointed to the lift tucked behind an opening on the right. This lift was small, slow and antiquated. Visitors with appointments to see officers of the company would take the lift to the first or second floor and emerge into a lofty, well-lighted passage where an attendant armed with a telephone would enquire their business. Having phoned the officer concerned the visitor would be invited to 'step this way please'. If the officer was not ready there was an adjoining Waiting Room, though initially, that on the second floor constituted the Board Room. Each of the four suites of offices (West Wing South on first/second floors and north corridors on the second and third floors) carried a polished name-board the names of BBC officers listed being written in gold shaded black.

Artistes would be directed to the third floor and shown into the Reception Room. At the appropriate time a few minutes before he or she was due to broadcast, the artiste would proceed to the studio suite perhaps spending a little time in the 'Green Room' before entering the studio proper .

After the performance, the Commissionaire, stationed in the Ante-Room, would open the stair door with a few brief words of encouragement and direction 'It came over very well, sir. There's the steps, sir; don't wait for the lift' (E. Alexander, op. cit.).

4.   NEW GENERAL OFFICE/SECOND STUDIO

SH-SUMMARY: Entries - 7 and 8: November 1923/February 1924.. Large room on second floor rented looking onto Embankment for new General Office; also large room on first floor facing Savoy Hotel for new studio premises. Workshops also rented in basement. New General Office and new large studio ready for use in January 1924 (Studio became known as No. 1 Studio).

This was the last major expansion within the IEE building on the part of the BBC but afforded only a few months respite. Nonetheless the acquisition of the South Wing provided a magnificent room 100ft long by 30ft and 18ft high with tall windows and a fine river view. Apart from offering a splendid General Office - a showpiece for the BBC - it also left space for a new Board Room, and offices for key BBC staff, in particular those concerned with administration and finance.

For the layout details within the South Wing we again have an unimpeachable source - a sketch plan by Reith dated 18 November 1923. The eastern portion of the South Wing, a space 38ft by 30ft, was reserved for typists being well-lit on both sides. The darker middle portion, about 25ft by 36ft deep and lit only on the south side, was the filing area. 15 years later it became a matter of wonder that in 1923 eleven girls were sufficient to cope with the filing of Savoy Hill (Goatman, p.27).

The filing area also served as a Post Room. This was staffed by 'Boys' who dealt with the post whether internal, incoming or outgoing. They arrived at 8.30 each morning, an hour in advance of the rest of the staff, to open and sort the first postal delivery. It was their job to attach the relevant papers to any letters referring to previous correspondence and they visited offices at regular intervals delivering to in trays and collecting from out-trays. The BBC had its own red GPO post-box: this was positioned on the main stair where it remained until 1993.

The western portion of the South Room was subdivided:

Room No. (at 1926)	Relevant Use/ Post	Name of Officer
South Wing, Second Floor (anti-clockwise from south west)		
12	Board Room	
13	Company Secretary	Rice
14	Registrar	Page
(Filing/Gen. Office Access)		(Miss Banks)
15	Cashier	Miss Mallinson
15A	Accountant	Harley

The officers and the clerical staff had a newly formed passageway to the stairs, the Managing Director and Controller retaining their own exclusive corridor to the lift. From the Managing Director's office there was direct access to the Board Room as well as access from there to the Company Secretary's room. Next to the Managing Director's office, Room 8 now housed Carpendale's secretary as well as Reith's.

The Cashier, Miss Mallinson, who had previously shared the Accountant's room, now had her own. Likewise, Page who was at last able to have a partition between his space and 'the roar of the typewriters'. Harley and his secretary (Miss Lock) vacated Room 4 which, with Rooms 1, 2 and 3 became the corridor for senior engineers, Room 4 being for the research and development heads - West and Kirke. Into Rooms 1 and 2 went Carter, R. H. Eckersley and Miss Fortune, where they danced attendance on the Chief Engineer, P. P. Eckersley (R. H. Eckersley, pp. 56/57). In Room - 3, Bishop and Litt were soon joined by Hayes.

A minute of January 1924 probably intended for the next Board Meeting and bearing Reith's authoritative style has survived.* This discusses the future use of the old General Office. Should senior Programme staff move in? Reith pointed out that top programme staff like Burrows, Lewis and Smith (Press and Publicity) needed sound proof offices - not space in an 18ft high room divided by part-height partitions. He turned his attention to the third floor, North Wing, where the Music Department and 2LO competed for space and decided the latter should move into the old General Office. Following its conversion, space was allocated in April :

---

* This minute helped the author to clarify the changes made earlier in September 1923 in the North Wing.

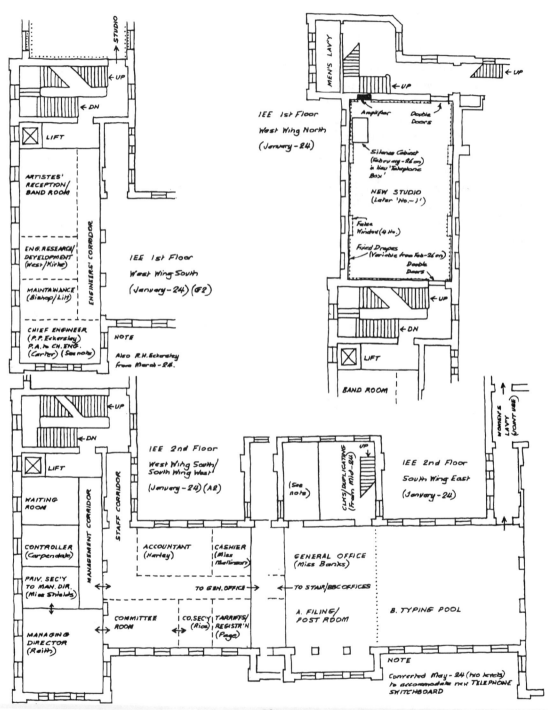

IEE 1st Floor
West Wing North
(January – 24)

↑ STUDIO
← UP
← DN
LIFT

ARTISTES'
RECEPTION/
BAND ROOM

ENG. RESEARCH/
DEVELOPMENT
(West/Kirke)

MAINTAINANCE
(Bishop/Litt)

CHIEF ENGINEER
(P.P. Eckersley)
P.A. to CH. ENG.
(Carter) (See note)

ENGINEERS' CORRIDOR

IEE 1st Floor
West Wing South
(January – 24) (G2)

NOTE

Also R.H. Eckersley
from March – 24.

Amplifier   Double
                 Doors

Silence Cabinet
(February – 26 on)
in New 'Telephone
Box'

NEW STUDIO
(Later 'No. – 1')

False
Windows (4 No.)

Fixed Drapes
(Variable from Feb – 26 on)
                 Double
                 Doors

MEN'S LAVY
← UP
← UP
← UP
← DN
LIFT

BAND ROOM

↑ UP
← DN
LIFT

WAITING
ROOM

CONTROLLER
(Carpendale)

PRIV. SEC'Y
TO MAN. DIR.
(Miss Shields)

MANAGING
DIRECTOR
(Reith)

MANAGEMENT CORRIDOR

STAFF CORRIDOR

IEE 2nd Floor
West Wing South/
South Wing West
(January – 24) (A2)

ACCOUNTANT
(Harley)

CASHIER
(Miss
Mullineer)

COMMITTEE
ROOM

CO. SEC'Y
(Rice)

TARRIFFS/
REGISTR'N
(Page)

TO GEN. OFFICE

(See
note)

CUTS/DUPLICATING
(From Mid – 24)

↑ UP

IEE 2nd Floor
South Wing East
(January – 24)

WOMEN'S
LAVY
(CAN'T USE)

GENERAL OFFICE
(Miss Banks)

← TO STAIR/BBC OFFICES

A. FILING/
POST ROOM

B. TYPING POOL

NOTE

Converted May – 24 (two levels)
to accommodate new TELEPHONE
SWITCHBOARD

Room No. (at 1926)	Relevant Use/ Post	Name of Officer
G.O. Room A	Director - 2LO	Palmer
B	2LO Prog. Staff	Dodgson/Wright
C	2LO Engineers/OB Eng.	Shaw/Thompson etc
D	Radio Times	Parker/Miss Bryant
24	Spare for Music Dept. (See Section 5 below)	
25	Controller/Dir.Music	P. T. Pitt /Jefferies/Mrs Wood
26	Music Department	Braithwaite /Robinson/Howgill
27/27A	Music Library	Hook/Miss Wright

Room - B would however soon be packed to capacity. In May, Dan Godfrey arrived from the Manchester 2ZY Station to become 2LO's new Director of Music and the first full-time conductor of the 2LO Wireless Orchestra. He was joined in September by Stanford Robinson who was transferred from the Music Department to 2LO to take over the new BBC Chorus. Meanwhile Broadbent joined Dodgson to provide a second full-time 2LO Announcer.* The fact that the announcers alternated doubtless helped to relieve over-crowding in Room - B.

The move of the old amplifier and the 2LO engineers from Room 24 in April (see Section - 5 below) meant that the whole of the third floor North Wing was now available to the Music Department. Pitt and Jefferies now had a decent office for themselves and their assistant, Mrs Wood. In the next room was Jefferies'

talented young Deputy, Warwick Braithwaite, who would shortly be transferred to Cardiff. He shared with Richard Howgill who had been appointed in December 1923 to manage the important Copyright Section. Robinson presumably continued in Room - 26 pending his transfer in September 1924 to 2LO. Hook's tiny Music Library in Room 27A could now expand into Room - 27 using shelving already in place.

On the second floor, North Wing, further changes were afoot in April 1924. In September, Wade had been allowed to stay on in Room - 17 where Lewis, Beadle and Miss Minns, played 'Happy Families'. Wade now joined Mrs Fitzgerald (Women's Hour) and Miss Elliott (Children's Hour) in Room - 16, after the departure of Parker and Miss Bryant. With more space and quieter habitat, he forthwith formed a new 'Programme Correspondence Department', as from 19 May. Its job was to answer with care the hundred letters a day which flooded into the BBC about programmes. For his part Burrows was left undisturbed in Room - 18, but Smith had to share Room - 19 with the new 'Artistic Director' - Corbett Smith - who was transferred to London from Cardiff where he had been Station Director. Reith was anxious the Artistic Director should have a room of his own and, in May, this became possible with the move of the Telephone Switchboard from

* Broadbent was in turn replaced by Stuart Hibberd in November 1924. A year or so later, Hibberd took over as Chief Announcer beginning his outstanding career as the 'Voice of Britain'.

Second Studio (later Studio 1) IEE Building, 1924 *(reproduced by permission of the Marconi Company, Ltd.)*

Room - 20 to a larger space in the new General Office.

In 1923 the two operators in the tiny Telephone Room at the end of the North Corridor handled 25,000 local out-going calls and 20,000 incoming (Goatman, p.32). The seven telephone lines were heavily overloaded. More lines, more operators and more space were all badly needed. Miss May (later Mrs Bottle) was in charge, and her prayers must have been heard for the central stairway adjoining the General Office was converted at enormous expense creating a space 24ft by 20ft on two levels and into this the new 10 - line switchboard

moved, a single telephone number - REGent 6730 - being adopted (Burrows, p.107 refers). This extension to the General Office probably housed the Duplicating Room where a roneo machine or two ground out memos and where people hung up their hats and coats (Ruth Cockerton writing in *Ariel (BBC House Magazine)* June 1938).

The creation of the new General Office had its parallel in the creation of a new larger, loftier studio. It took up the whole of the first floor North Room, a space 44ft long, 26ft wide and 18ft high. It could accommodate the Wireless Orchestra, about twenty three strong, with ease and had room for an augmented orchestra together with chorus and principals (Burrows, p. 97). The studio was directly over the Institution's Council Chamber. In consequence, the lease banned its use for broadcasting or rehearsals whilst IEE Council meetings were in progress.

The interior of the studio was much less claustrophobic than that of the older studio up on the third floor. The walls were lined with only a single layer of hessian behind grey drapes. On each of the longer walls two full-length 'windows' were created and fitted with curtains of a beautiful emerald shade. The windows could not be looked through for they had a background of silver foil in front of which hung an orange-coloured network. Surrounding the windows but hidden by the green curtains were numerous electric lamps which, when switched on, gave an effect of golden sunlight entering the room. But the lights were rarely used as they generated too much heat. The studio contained two grand pianos, one at each end, which differed in their musical "brilliancy" and so offered a choice to performers (Burrows, p.89).

Like the earlier studio, Studio - I had red lights positioned over the doors at each end. To achieve sound-proofing, duplicate sets of doors were provided and the outer doors also had red lights over. Moreover similar lights were fitted to the north and south entrances to the second floor room directly above to warn their occupants not to thump on the floor when broadcasting from Studio - I was in progress, this being indicated

by the red lamps being turned on so they glowed brightly (Burrows, p. 91). The old pair of doors to the north end of the second floor room still bear the original plaque with its invocation - 'PLEASE WALK QUIETLY WHEN RED LIGHT IS ON'.

Unlike the original studio, Studio - I had no Operator's Room, adjacent Waiting Room or Amplifier Room. The positioning of artistes and instrumentalists relative to the microphone was undertaken, often during rehearsals, by the producer of the programme. To do this properly, he needed to listen through headphones sitting in comparative silence so the final broadcast via microphone and amplifier could be judged and any faults in balance corrected. To enable him to do this an ordinary telephone cabinet was placed in the studio. It was equipped with a telephone to enable the producer to contact the Control Room when that room became established in April (A. G. D. West. *Wireless World*. 2 March 1927).

The availability of two studios meant that a first move towards specialisation became possible with the older studio being used for the spoken word and the newer for orchestral programmes. There was often time, before the performance, to get everybody into place. A reception/waiting/band room was still needed; but it did not have to immediately adjoin the studio. Space on the far side of the stair was probably used for this purpose, echoing the 3rd floor arrangements. The only problem was lack of heating for artistes at weekends.

From April 1924, Studio - 1, like Studio - 3 on the third floor, used the new Marconi 'A' microphone amplifier linked to a 'B' amplifier in the Control Room. The 'A' amplifier needed no attention and was small enough to be housed within the thickness of the north wall of Studio - 1 set behind a glazed door. In the first two or three months, Studio - 1 had probably employed the Western Electric 'double button' microphone and amplifier then much in vogue in BBC studios and used in London for outside broadcasts. Like the new Marconi amplifier, the Western Electric amplifier was wall-mounted and could fit in a small space.

5. CONTROL ROOM AND 'R AND D' WORKSHOPS

SH - SUMMARY: (See Entry - 7): February and April 1924. A major re-organisation of engineering arrangements occurred in this period which included the last stage in the occupation of IEE space by the BBC. On 28 February 1924 the IEE Finance Committee reported to the IEE Council that the IEE had let to the BBC two rooms on the west side of the Basement for £120 p.a.

For a year the Marconi Sykes microphone - the 'Magnetophone' had relied on the big, temperamental amplifier developed in pre-Savoy Hill days. By April 1924 a new method of control had been developed using two stages of amplification, first a small 'A' amplifier positioned close to the microphone and needing little attention; and secondly an equally small 'B' amplifier which required constant attention but which could be positioned some distance from the studio. This development immediately opened the way to grouping the control and SB equipment in one room - the 'Control Room'

At the same time, R and D work was expanding with a Deputy Chief Engineer in charge assisted, from February 1924, by a new Head of Development. Much more workshop space was required on the third floor, the one bay being totally inadequate. The solution was for the Engineering Department to take over the whole of the South Room with a sequence of rooms for Research, Control Room (two bays) and Development in that order (Pawley, pp. 54/55). The Auditions Room became the new Control

Control room, 1924

Room the ceiling being removed. The beautiful Reception Room, only seven months in use, was sacrificed for R & D.

The loss of the Auditions Room to amplifier/SB use was compensated by the move of the 2LO engineers and the old amplifier from Room 24 of the North Wing. Room 24 became the new Auditions Room and provided overflow space for Studio - 3's artistes.

The 'A' amplifier was mounted in the Operator's Room to serve Studio - 3, with another in the thickness of the north wall of Studio - 1. The 'B' amplifier in the Control Room was desk-mounted with an Input Board on one side and an Output Board on the other. The Input Board allowed the Control Engineer to select the Programme source. Sources included one or other of the two Savoy Hill studios, the Big Ben and Greenwich time signals,* and any one of about 75 Outside Broadcast points such as the London theatres. The Output Board was for programme destination routing to the London transmitter, the Control Room's SB board, or both (West, p. 13).

Two control desks were provided, the second serving as a stand by or allowing overlap. For example, the studio announcer's "Goodnight; goodnight, everybody", could be accompanied by dance music faded in from an OB point like the Savoy Hotel, the music then continuing long after the studio had closed for the night. The new control desks came into operation on 1 April. Meanwhile the old amplifier was moved fifty feet or so from the North Wing to the vicinity of the Control Room where

it was retained for a few months as a stand-by till confidence in the new amplifiers built up (P. P. Eckersley, *Radio Times*, 11 & 25 April 1924).

The second task was to move the SB Board from the Development Workshop to the Control Room. The new Board was much larger: it had to incorporate the new main stations at Bournemouth and Aberdeen and the growing number of Relay Stations in other cities. These Relay Stations took their programmes from the Main Stations, in particular, from 2LO. The new SB Board was on the west wall; the amplifiers against the other walls; against the fourth wall a receiver was provided to check the 2LO transmissions.

The creation of the Control Room meant a massive re-wiring task involving practically the whole of the broadcasting circuits at Savoy Hill. It had to be completed without any break in programme transmission. It was an all-night job which left little scope for tidiness. Moreover there was a prospect of further growth and upheaval. So the Control Room remained in a Heath Robinson state of improvisation until November 1925 when further expansion occurred but resulting, this time, in an orderly and efficient layout which served for the remaining Savoy Hill years.

The Engineering Division did not confine itself to the first and third floors of the West Wing: it also took space in

* The time signal of 'pips' relayed from Greenwich was introduced on a daily basis on 5 February 1924. A little later, on 9 March, a daily service of Big Ben chimes was inaugurated, the latter replacing the Announcer's nightly solo performance on the tubular bells.

the basement. Here the South Room (West Wing) was allocated to Central Stores use whilst the North Room served as a Workshop. Access was by lift from the main BBC entrance though the Workshop could also be approached through the archway at No. 4 Savoy Hill and down the slope of the little carriageway.

(reproduced by permission of the BBC)

An audition at 2LO, February, 1927

6. BBC'S EXPANSION WITHIN IEE BUILDING: 1923/24

In less than a year the BBC had come to occupy all the available space in the Institution building. This space was concentrated in the West and North Wings but included the South Wing, second floor. The ground floor was largely in Institution use and the South Wing, first floor, was occupied by the Institution's library. The East Wing had already been leased to other organisations when the BBC first approached the IEE.

As has been shown, the BBC occupation occurred in a number of stages and the negotiations with the IEE and subsequent leasing arrangements are summarised in this Section. In order to do this we need to go right back to 1922. The Institution's representative at that time was P. F. Rowell, who had been the IEE Secretary from 1909, when they first moved into the building and adapted the lecture hall for institutional use. The BBC's representative was John Reith, the General Manager, whose first two days of BBC work had been spent in the search for suitable, low cost premises resulting in his decision to go for Savoy Hill.

Initial negotiations had already started before Reith's appointment and even before the establishment of the BBC. In August 1922, Sir William Noble who headed the Broadcasting Committee,* was already in touch with Rowell with regard to accommodation for the future BBC. Rowell offered the South Wing second floor at £1,000 p.a.

By November 1922 the BBC had been formed, but the Broadcasting Committee still continued to act for it as there were, as yet, no staff. Two of its members, Binyon and Isaacs, met Gill, who was President of the IEE and Rowell, the Secretary. Having sketched some accommodation needs literally on the back of an envelope, they decided that, in addition to the South Wing, the adjoining South Room in the West Wing would be needed. The combined rent would be £1,400 p.a. and Noble was advised to accept this offer. But he held back.

Burrows, too, was to turn his footsteps in the direction of Savoy Hill. At the time (September/October 1922) he was in charge of the 2LO experimental station as Programme Manager, the Engineering responsibility falling on another Marconi Officer - R. H. White. Burrows in his official capacity was Publicity Officer for Marconi's but he had built up an unrivalled knowledge and understanding of what broadcasting was all about along with a remarkable vision as to where it might lead.

Unlike the others he went with a clear idea as to BBC staffing at the future Head Office. There would be a Director of Programmes, a Musical Director, a Provincial Programme Director responsible for artistes touring the various BBC stations, and a Supervising Engineer. Each would have an Assistant. In addition, the BBC would need a publicity chief and a business manager combining the roles of the Company Secretary and Accountant. Burrows added a 'Lady Assistant' to help develop programmes of interest to women. The general supporting staff would include two programme announcers, six typists, five clerks to take care of filing and Roneo copying, two messengers, and two Commissionaires - for the BBC would be active early in the morning and late at night, its doors open every day of the week.

Burrows, unlike the earlier visitors, was interested in the ten rooms comprising the North Wing; ready-made offices available for immediate occupation. All were 12ft deep, six were 20ft wide, two were 12ft wide and two more 7ft. He also examined a room 44ft by 27ft on the top floor and decided it would make an excellent setting for the studio (or 'concert room' as he called it) especially as it was large enough to allow space for waiting artistes. He judged right: in due course it became the 2LO studio. All

* The Committee was made up of leading representatives of the six companies mainly concerned with financing the BBC and constructing its transmitting stations - Marconi, Metropolitan Vickers, Radio Communication, Western Electric, General Electric and British Thomson-Houston. The Committee negotiated with the Postmaster General, press and other interests the creation of the BBC

eleven rooms were available at £850 p.a. and Burrows recommended they be taken. Again, the Broadcasting Committee held back.

But the Committee were prepared to attack the question of staff. In October 1922 four posts were advertised and on the 13 December action was at last taken. In the beautiful second floor Board Room at Magnet House, Kingsway, short-listed candidates were interviewed for four key posts - Company Secretary, General Manager, Director of Programmes and Chief Engineer. The posts were offered to Anderson, Reith, Arthur Burrows with Cecil Lewis as his Deputy, and R. H. White the Marconi engineer responsible with Burrows for 2LO, the London Station.*

Over the following weekend, having sorted out his own future and salary, Reith discussed the staff needed for the new enterprise with the only man who could advise - Arthur Burrows. On the Monday, having at least some ideas as to staff numbers, he turned his attention to the matter of accommodation. The search party met on the pavement at the bottom of Kingsway opposite Bush House - four men, one 6ft 4in and another even taller with 'a sort of lofty detachment surrounding him'. There was no mistaking this man - John Reith, the new General Manager, BBC (Cecil Lewis, *Never Look Back*, published by Hutchinson, London, 1974 p. 64). Reith was accompanied by Noble, Burrows and Lewis (the other tall man). They examined a number of sites for the new BBC Head Office without much success.

On the following day, the search was resumed only this time Reith, Burrows and Lewis were accompanied by White. Each site seemed worse than the last. Reith gives us a vivid account of what then transpired:

'Finally, as dusk was falling, we came to Savoy Hill. It seemed the worst of all. First we had to locate and interview the caretaker of the Institution of Electrical Engineers. Yes, the Institution had large premises vacant in their block with separate entries and so on. Being instructed by him to present ourselves at another door, the game, so to speak, began. Having circumambulated the block, we composed ourselves before one gloomy portal to attend till such time as, by devious underground channels, the caretaker might reasonably be expected to arrive at the same entrance, but on the other side of it. This, in due course, he in fact did, but it was apparently not the intended rendezvous, for no entrance was obtained. It is difficult to receive geographical directions from behind a solid door, and in this case it was quite unsatisfactory. There were many other doors. Finally, however, the two parties succeeded in arriving simultaneously at opposite sides of the   same openable door, and we were admitted. What a depressing place it was. It had been used for some   mysterious   LCC   medical activities,   vacated   some   months

*   R.H. White did not take up the post and it was subsequently offered to Peter Eckersley.

earlier, and much dirt and depression had accumulated since then. It was difficult to see any convenient arrangement for studios, etc., on the one hand or offices on the other. (But) if ever the windows at the end of one vast chamber could be made transparent a fine river panorama would be obtainable.' (Reith as quoted in Allighan, pp. 179/180).

The vast chamber was the South Room, West Wing on the second floor. The windows in due course became those of Reith's room and afforded 'one of the finest views in town'.

The Victorian accommodation with its great 18ft high rooms was not convenient for office use but the building afforded several key advantages:

It was close to the transmitter at Marconi House pending erection of masts at the IEE;

It provided independent access for BBC use at No. 2 Savoy Hill both by stair and by a handy, if antiquated, lift;

The solid walled, windowless top floor could be used for studio and workshops;

And, most importantly, there appeared to be ample space for future growth.

The Institution of Electrical Engineers was, in a sense, an allied body and its Secretary was sympathetic to the needs of the fledgling BBC. Even at this stage Reith may have felt that an institutional home would prove desirable in that it would reflect the public service ethos of the BBC rather than its less exalted commercial roots. To Burrows and

Lewis, responsible for news, talks, music and entertainment, the IEE's proximity to Fleet Street and to theatrical and music agents were points in its favour. For White, the ability of the building's roof to support two 100ft masts to carry the transmitter aerial would have to be checked but, if all else failed, he could use his influence with his old colleagues to retain the temporary use of the Marconi House transmitter. A short land-line could connect the two buildings (West, p. 8). The IEE's backwater site would at least reduce the problem of sound proofing the studio and amplifier room.

Reith accordingly met Rowell the next day. It was decided the BBC would take the West Wing, second floor, comprising two large rooms: also the North Wing, second floor which afforded five offices. The north room in the West Wing on the top floor was also included: this was to be the studio. Permission for the IEE to sub-let only came on 7 March 1923 from the Savoy Estate and the lease was hurriedly rushed through on 15 March only four days before the BBC moved in! The rent, including rates and heating, was to be £1,200 p.a. (Appleyard, pp. 257/258).

But whilst the arrangements enabled the 31 Head Office staff and their General Manager to be housed in sub-divided and redecorated space, it made no allowance for the 2LO staff at Marconi House, nor for the proposed music department. A revised lease was quickly prepared which added the large Southern rooms in the West Wing's first and third floors: and, in addition, the third floor of the North Wing. The new agreement, covering a two-year period, replaced the earlier one and a new rent was fixed at £2,050 p.a.

In the event, the first floor space was not taken until 7 September 1923 and, in the meantime, the rent was reduced to £1,600 p.a. payable quarterly commencing in arrears at the end of June. The agreement included use of the lavatories on the west and north-west stairs. There was provision for joint use of the lavatories on the north-east stair and the little lavatory adjoining the South Room, third floor, was also available for BBC use.* The lift at the No. 2 Savoy Hill entrance was to be for BBC use exclusively, but operated during normal working hours by an IEE lift attendant.

In November 1923 a further lease was prepared, this time to cover a ten-year period and to include the huge room that formed the second floor, South Wing. The rent would increase by £1,000: but the first floor North Room was included to provide a second studio with the proviso that its use for broadcasting should not interfere with meetings in the IEE's Council Chamber, immediately below. In February 1924 the IEE let two rooms on the west side of the Basement to the BBC at £120 annually bringing the total rent payable to £3,170 (Appleyard, p. 258). Finally, in May 1924, the old central stair from the second to the third floor was converted by the BBC to provide a small extension to the General Office on its north side. The annualrent was fixed at a nominal £25. Overall, this gave the BBC about

13,000 sq.ft (excluding the Base-ment, stairs and lavatories), the best space letting for about 30/35p per square foot.

But, over and above rental charges, the BBC faced considerable conversion, redecoration, wiring and furniture expenses. Economies had to be made; for example, some of the tall echoey rooms on the first and second floors were sub-divided by flimsy 11 ft partitions glazed at the top: staff were, in effect, packed into 'loose-boxes' (Snagge/Barsley, p.3).

* Joint use must have added to the problems of blockages and breakages. Reith tried to ensure BBC staff were not responsible by condemning in no uncertain terms the rubbish found deposited in cisterns, urinals and wash-basins such as small pieces of paper, orange peel and cigarette butts.

2LO transmitter in Selfridges, 1925
(reproduced by permission of the Marconi Company, Ltd.)

SAVOY HILL MANSIONS

1. EXPANSION BEYOND IEE BUILDING

SH-SUMMARY: Entry - 9: Summer 1924. Lease taken of north-west corner of block-formerly a block of flats destroyed by a bomb during the War and never rebuilt.

By mid-1924 there were at least 150 staff squeezed into the BBC's space and that was about the limit (Reith, pp. 36/37). It was urgently necessary both to plan boldly for future growth and to find some kind of interim solution however inconvenient this might be.

Solution lay with Savoy Hill Mansions, a six-storey building which backed on to the IEE. The building had however one major problem: its western wing had been destroyed in a Zeppelin raid in 1917. This part would require complete reconstruction and, until then, the Mansions would afford no direct access from the BBC's existing space in the West and North Wings of the IEE. But reconstruction would at once open up the opportunity for the BBC to expand into the whole of Savoy Hill Mansions via connecting internal passageways.

Accordingly, on 29 August 1924, a lease was taken on the bombed Western Wing. The plan then was to build a replica of what was there before - at least as to external appearances - and to take over the remaining undamaged portion of the Mansions. To distinguish the reconstructed corner from the rest of the Mansions we will use the term 'North West Building'.

2. TEMPORARY OCCUPATION OF MANSIONS

SH-SUMMARY: Entries - 10 and 11: August 1924/January 1925. Eight rooms on first floor of Bath Stores (i.e. 18 Savoy Street) rented for use while corner building was being rebuilt (August 1924). Rented whole of Second Floor (January 1925).

A number of entries in the *Savoy Hill Summary* refer to 'Bath Stores' or 'Bath Buildings'. No. 18 Savoy Street was, occupied by T. Bath, Contractors, and, by a strange coincidence, had previously been occupied by a Turkish Baths establishment. That 'Bath Stores/Buildings' was synonymous with Savoy Hill Mansions is clear from Entry 13 which refers to 'leasing the whole of the building as far as the portion being rebuilt'. The reference to '18 Savoy Street' is to the eastern entrance to the Mansions. This entrance served not only the commercial uses on the lower floors but afforded access to flats on the upper floors. The western entrance, which had likewise faced the Chapel Royal church-yard, had been destroyed by bombing but was being rebuilt as part of the new North West Building project.

The urgent need to take up temporary accommodation arose from the creation of two new departments within the Programme Division, one for drama headed by Jeffrey and the other for talks and education under Stobart, Jeffrey having been transferred to Savoy Hill in July 1924 and Stobart having taken up his post in August. There was more-over a third department within the

Programme Division needing more space. In May 1924 the Programme Correspondence section under Ralph Wade was started up to cope with the flood of letters - some 20,000 a year (By 1926 this figure had increased to 30,000) (*BBC Handbook* for 1928, p. 336).

The First Floor of the Mansions comprised about a dozen rooms and it is difficult now to be sure which were occupied and by whom but the following officers would have taken up office space in the period from August 1924 to June 1925 when temporary occupation ended:

Relevant Use/ Post	Name of Officer	From
Dir. Educ/Talks	Stobart	Aug, 24
Educ/Talks	Broadbent	Nov, 24
Prog. Correspondence	R. Wade	Aug, 24
Dir. Drama	Jeffrey	Aug, 24
Producer Plays	Rose	Jan, 25
Dramatic Effects	Whitman	Nov, 24
Rehearsal Room	-	Aug, 24

It is likely that the Outside Broadcasts Section also transferred to the Mansions during the period of temporary occupation - August 1924 to June 1925. The Head of the OB Unit, R. H. Eckersley, who had joined the BBC in February 1924, wrote later how he was soon given an office to share with his secretary (Miss Jockel) and an expert engineer (Thompson) (Eckersley, p. 57).

These same departments may have spread after January 1925 into the second floor as they expanded. They had ample space, but they were almost wholly isolated from the rest of the BBC staff and management. Entry to their offices could only be effected by going out of the front door (the BBC's main entrance at No. 2 Savoy Hill) and walking right round to the East Entrance (*i.e.* No. 18 Savoy Street). Here, after braving the care-taker's dog, and getting rather a fright from the head of a bison hung on the wall in a dark passage, one found the dramatists and educationalists aloof in their secluded quarters. (*BBC Year-Book* 1930, p. 171).

3. OCCUPATION OF UPPER PART OF MANSIONS

SH-SUMMARY: Entries - 12 to 16: April/ September 1925. Rented two rooms on fourth floor (April 1925). Occupied fifth floor with the whole of third and fourth floors in placeof second and first floor accommodation (June 1925). Accepted offer of lease of the whole of the building as far as the portion being rebuilt as from June 1926 (May 1925). The two top floors and basement of new corner building occupied, and through access to 2 Savoy Hill made on third and fourth floors (September 1925). BBC premises to be known simply as 'Savoy Hill' which would cover the three buildings and the old title of '2 Savoy Hill' (to) be dropped. Now two entrances: West Entrance, and North Entrance in new block (September 1925).

The new title 'Savoy Hill' applied to the whole of the premises occupied by the BBC at September 1925. The 'West Entrance' was the original at No. 2 Savoy Hill which formed part of the IEE premises. The 'North Entrance' gave general BBC access to the Mansions at its reconstructed western end.

DRAWN BY OUR SPECIAL ARTIST, C. E. TURNER. (COPYRIGHTED.)

Variety Studio, North West Building: Illustrated London News, 13 April, 1929

(reproduced by permission of the Illustrated London News Picture Library)

The East Entrance continued in use, but visitors used only the North and West Entrances as appropriate.

The change in title reflected not only the creation of new entrances but the change in emphasis from the IEE Building to the Mansions. The lease on the Mansions was taken on the 8 July 1925 and provided the use of the third, fourth and fifth floors as from 25 June 1925. The lower floors still had some old tenants and would require substantial gutting and internal reconstruction to create new studios. It was envisaged that they would only be ready for occupation from mid-1926. Meantime the staff on the first and second floors now had to transfer to the upper floors of the Mansions.

But this was merely a prelude to a fundamental and permanent change in the BBC's internal organisation and departmental disposition.

The period June to September 1925 saw the biggest shake-up of BBC staff that ever occurred in 'Company' days. The office space permanently available to the BBC more than doubled and pressures for space due to growth in the number of staff would have ensured quick take-up of the new accommodation. As it was, the temporary allocation of space had only just kept pace with demand. This becomes apparent if we compare staff numbers with the space becoming available at each stage:

NB. Staff numbers are based on Head Office/2LO numbers known to exist in September 1924 and in May 1926 (Reith, pp. 36/37: Briggs - I, p. 367: Allighan, p. 195).

DATE	ACCOM (Offices)	AREA (SQ.FT)	NO. STAFF	SQ.FT PERSON (Estimated)
Dec, 23	IEE Building	5750	90	65
Jan, 24	IEE Building	8750	100	87*
Aug, 24	ditto plus First Fl. (Mansions)	10750	165	65
Jan, 25	ditto plus 2nd Fl. (Mansions)	13800	210	65
Jun, 25	IEE Bdg. plus 3rd, 4th, 5th Floors (Mansions)	16000	245	65
Sep, 25	ditto plus 3rd, 4th floors North West Bdg.	18700	270	69

Given some 65/69 sq. ft per employee, no less than 150 staff would have moved into the upper floors of Savoy Hill Mansions in the summer of 1925 and additional staff would have been moved into the space vacated by those moves, space which, as we shall see, existed mainly in the North Wing of the IEE building. This space amounts to over 2,000 sq. ft - equivalent to a further 30 staff. In short, 180 staff, two thirds of the total, took up new accommodation in the summer of 1925.

It seems highly improbable that these moves of existing staff and the location of new staff would have been haphazard. Grouping by division and department would surely have occurred. These assumptions are supported by a surviving Staff Directory of 1926. This is examined

* The acquisition of the South Wing, IEE second floor, added 3000 sq. ft of office space in January 1924 creating a temporary surplus.

in more detail in the next Section: it reveals clear links between divisions and floors/buildings:

BUILDING/ FLOOR — DIVISION DEPARTMENT

Mansions 5th Fl. Engineering
               Research/Devt.
Mansions 4th Fl. Information
               Publications
               Radio Times
               World Radio
               Photographic
               Library
               Press
         General Office
               Filing/Duplic'g
Mansions 3rd Fl.   Programmes
               Talks/Education
               Music
               Children's Hour
               London Station
               OBs
IEE 1st Fl.   Engineering
IEE 2nd Fl.   Secretariat
          Finance
          Management
          General
               Typing/Filing/Post
IEE 3rd Fl.   Engineering Equipment
               Technical Corresp.

The disposition of functional units shown above existed by late 1926 and would presumably have resulted from the initial move in the summer of 1925: (a double upheaval within a single year would be both pointless and unthinkable). But one department - Drama - did undergo a double move, leaving the first floor of the Mansions for an upper floor in June 1925 before descending in 1926 to ground level.

4. ROOM ALLOCATION IN MANSIONS

The *Savoy Hill Summary* gives no indication as to floor or room allocation in the Mansions and no sketch layouts equivalent to those showing room allocation in the IEE Building appear to have survived. But in the BBC Archives there is a Staff Directory listing names and room numbers, dated December 1926, covering both the IEE Building and the Mansions. This Directory is limited to senior staff and their secretaries.

The list shows names but not jobs so it is difficult to see how room numbers related to Divisions or Departments. Asa Briggs in *The Birth of Broadcasting* shows these Divisions for 1926 as an organisational chart at the rear of the volume; but the chart bears no names! The reconciliation of names and Divisions/Departments as at 1926 was however completed by the author using a variety of sources, not least Briggs. It was therefore possible to see how rooms and, in particular, specific groups of rooms were allocated to these departments. For example, rooms 47/60 all housed the Programmes Division. What was now needed was a set of plans showing these room numbers.

The Institution of Electrical Engineers have plans of their building dating from about 1908 when they first moved in. In addition, coloured plans show changes to the ground and first floors which occurred in 1909/10. Another set of plans shows further changes proposed in 1958. But there is none contemporary with the BBC period. However we know from the 1923 sketches (figs 11 and 14 above) which rooms were occupied by senior officers like Reith, Carpendale and P. P. Eckersley and they did not change their offices. The BBC Directory shows these rooms as Nos. 7, 9 and 1 respectively. It is clear from this that the numbering sequence began in the IEE building on the first floor from the southern end and continued with the second floor, again working from the south (Reith's room). Certain rooms lacked numbers, for example, the General Office, Post Room, and the Basement Stores and Workshop. It is possible that the two studios were unnumbered. But Waiting Rooms and the Board Room, although not identified in the Directory, were almost certainly numbered as gaps appear in the sequence just where one would expect to find these rooms. The number of rooms occupied by the BBC in the IEE Building was sufficient to account for about thirty of the hundred or so shown in the Directory. Staff in rooms numbered 30 upwards could therefore be assumed to occupy the Mansions.

The IEE Archives include plans of the surviving portion of the Mansions as it existed immediately prior to BBC occupation along with plans dated late - 1924 showing the proposed reconstruction of the North West Building. Strangely one plan, but only one plan, shows room numbers - the Mansions' ground floor plan. This shows a sequence from 90 to 98 but including a 'Room 95A'. The BBC Directory shows most of these as occupied viz: nos. 90, 91, 92, 94, 95A, 96 and 98. It also shows occupants who we know belonged to the Drama and Productions Department. Their presence on the ground floor of the Mansions is confirmed by Gorham in his book *Sound and Fury* (p.33). He refers to Sharman and Fryer of that Department, as being 'on the ground floor'. (They occupied Rooms 91 and 92).

The numbering of the Mansions must therefore have been from the top down reflecting the take-up of accommodation, the top floors being occupied earlier than the lower. This is again substantiated by Gorham (p.30) where he describes his 'long narrow room looking over the churchyard ... Our office was on the fourth floor and the window gave on to a wide cornice'. The Directory shows Gorham accommodated in Room 41 (He later moved into Room 40). Gorham refers to a formidable 'Miss B' round the corner, who also worked, like himself, on the *Radio Times*. This can be none other than Miss Bryant, the tough old hand who occupied Room 43*. This too is relevant as it suggests, as does the ground floor plan, a clockwise room numbering along the street front, round the corner and along the back of the block.

* The two main *Radio Times* rooms had windows facing east which, with the demolition of the Duchy of Lancaster Office and terrace about 1927, afforded a view of Somerset House (*BBC Year Book*, 1932, p.98).

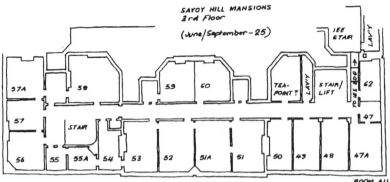

SAVOY HILL MANSIONS
3rd Floor

(June/September - 25)

SAVOY HILL MANSIONS (PROGRAMMES/2LO)

SH MANSIONS (NORTH WEST BDG.)
(PROGRAMMES)

ROOM ALLOCATION AT DECEMBER 1926

47:47A:48	HEAD/DEP. PROGRAMMES
49	PROGRAMMES EXECUTIVE
51:51A:52	TALKS/LOCAL NEWS/EDUCATION
53:54	2LO
55:55A	OUTSIDE BROADCASTS - 2LO
56:57:57A:58	MUSIC/CH.ANNOUNCER
59	CHILDREN'S HOUR
60	S.B./ANNOUNCER - 2LO
62	CONTROL ROOM ENGINEERS

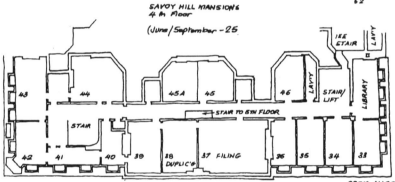

SAVOY HILL MANSIONS
4th Floor

(June/September - 25)

SAVOY HILL MANSIONS (RADIO TIMES/DRAMA(?))

S.H. MANSIONS (NORTH WEST BDG.)
(PRESS/INFORMATION)

ROOM ALLOCATION AT DECEMBER 1926

33:46	LIBRARY/PHOTO LIBRARY
34:35	HEAD/DEP. INFORMATION
36	PRESS
37:38	REGISTRY
39:46	PUBLICATIONS
40:44	INTERNATIONAL/'WORLD RADIO'
41:42:43	RADIO TIMES

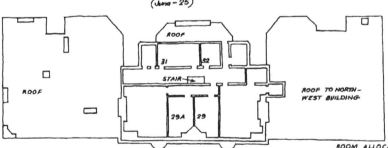

SAVOY HILL MANSIONS
5th Floor

(June - 25)

SAVOY HILL MANSIONS (ENGINEERING R.AND D)

ROOM ALLOCATION AT DECEMBER 1926

29:29A	ENGINEERING DEVELOPMENT
31:32(?)	ENGINEERING RESEARCH

The remaining question was to decide from what point the Mansions numbering commenced; did it in fact commence on the top (fifth) floor with Room - 30 as has been suggested above? Pawley, in his history of BBC engineering, provides a valuable clue. 'Research and Development Sections inhabited the attics of Savoy Hill (where) H. L. Kirke shared a small office with his assistant L. W. Hayes and his secretary ... Towards the end of 1927 Research and Development Sections moved to Avenue House, Kings Avenue, Clapham' (Pawley, p.198). The tiny fifth floor exactly fits the description 'attics' as it looked on to the roof of much of the fourth floor. The Directory shows Kirke and Hayes in Room 29A with Room 31 reserved for Research. Rooms 28, 29, 30 and 32 are not shown in the Directory but may also have been on the fifth floor. By contrast, Rooms 24, 25, 26, 27 and 27A, which are listed, refer to the North Wing (third floor) of the IEE Building where the end room (No. 27A) was entered from the neighbouring one (No. 27) rather than direct from the corridor. That the western room in the North Wing was numbered '24' is confirmed by a photograph of the Musical Control Room. The picture tallies uniquely with the western room, North Wing, and is captioned 'Room 24'. The IEE room sequence therefore must have finished with Room 27A.

The plans of the Mansions can thus be annotated with room numbers starting with '28' and working from the top downward, each floor being numbered clockwise starting with the street frontage and finishing round the back.

The annotated Directory can then be drawn on to fit names to rooms; and jobs to names. The results are shown in Appendix - D and it is clear from this that, not surprisingly, rooms and occupants were grouped by Division and by Department. Moreover a simple relationship between floors and Divisions emerged:

FLOOR	ROOM NO. IN DIRECTORY	DIVISION
5th Fl.	29A/31	Engineering (R and D Dept.)
4th Fl.	33/46	Information
3rd Fl.	47/60	Programmes (but exc. Drama Dept.)

The new 'Assistant Controllers' heading Information and Programmes Divisions both occupied new offices in the North West Building where they enjoyed easy access both to the lift and, via a new linking passageway, to the Management Suite and to the other three Assistant Controllers in the IEE Building.

It was probably at the end of 1925 that the numbering of rooms was adopted by the BBC. Apart from its room number, each door had a piece of pasteboard fixed to it with a drawing pin and bearing the names and department of the room's occupants. It was not a very attractive solution but typical of the Savoy Hill approach which was to improvise. It was also practical for some departments were, even as late as December 1925, still in temporary accommodation pending the creation of offices on the lower floors of the Mansions.

5. STUDIOS - 2, 4 AND 5 IN NORTH WEST BUILDING

SH-SUMMARY: Entry - 17: Autumn 1925/ December 1925. Two studios opened in new corner block, known as No. 2 and No. 4, the latter being immediately under No. 2. Also small Talks Studio, No. 5, opposite No. 4.

Plans of the North West Building have been preserved in the archives of the IEE. They were prepared in the autumn of 1924 by Mewes and Davis, architects, and show the following accommodation:

FLOOR	CHURCHYARD FRONTAGE	SAVOY HILL FRONTAGE	ISOLATED REAR ROOM
3rd/4th	4 Offices	Office	Office
2nd	2 Rehearsal Rms	Auditions	Band Room
1st	Large Studio	Green Room	Small Talks Studio
Grd.	Waiting Room / North Entrance / Spare Room	Spare Room	Enquiries
B'ment	Canteen/Kitchen	Boiler House	Unallocated

It is clear from the *SH-Summary* above that ideas for the second floor changed in favour of a studio designed for drama productions - Studio - 2. This was a three-room complex, one of the 'rehearsal rooms' becoming the Effects Room while the other became the studio proper. Leading back along Savoy Hill, the 'auditions room' became an Echo Room leading off the studio through communicating doors. The sounds reaching the Echo Room from the studio were picked up on a microphone and then mixed in with that from the microphones in the studio or the Effects Room (West, p.12). The play's producer occupied a tiny soundproof cabinet overlooking the Studio and Effects Room and had his own microphone for announcements and for giving directions to performers equipped with earphones (A. G. D. West, *Wireless World*, 23 February 1927).

The ability to blend sound from different rooms was an important step forward. By using background sounds and varying the reverberation the producer could add atmosphere and 'location' to drama with contrasts between indoor and outdoor effects. According to Gielgud who succeeded Jeffrey as Head of BBC drama, Howard Rose, who became the chief producer July 1925, was probably the first to use the 'little black box with two control-knobs, each of which was linked to a separate microphone on either side of a glass panel dividing (the) studio from the Effects Room. Against the side of this screen was partitioned off a tiny cubicle with just enough room to

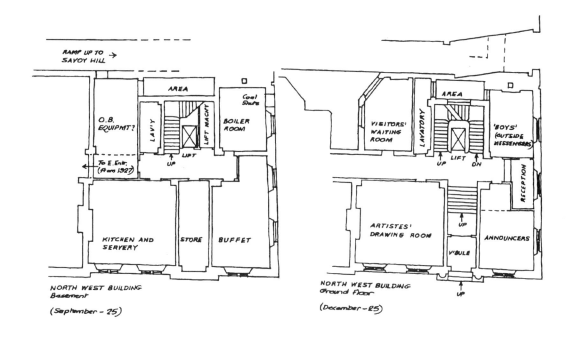

RAMP UP TO →
SAVOY HILL

AREA

Coal
Shute

O.B.
EQUIPMT?

LAV'Y

LIFT MACH'Y

BOILER
ROOM

LIFT

UP

To E.Entr.
(from 1927)

KITCHEN AND
SERVERY

STORE

BUFFET

NORTH WEST BUILDING
Basement

(September – 25)

VISITORS'
WAITING
ROOM

AREA

LAVATORY

'BOYS'
(OUTSIDE
MESSENGERS)

LIFT

UP

DN

RECEPTION

ARTISTES'
DRAWING ROOM

UP

ANNOUNCERS

V'BULE

NORTH WEST BUILDING
Ground Floor

UP

(December – 25)

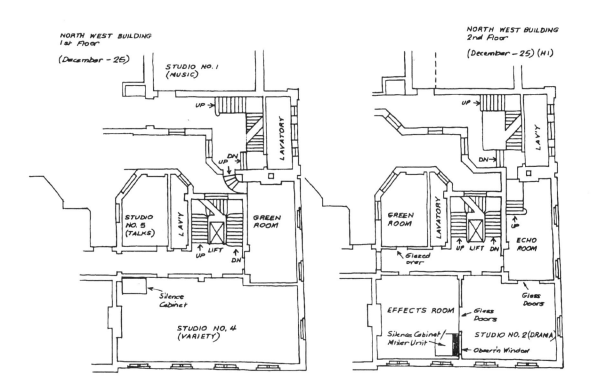

NORTH WEST BUILDING
1st Floor

(December – 25)

STUDIO NO. 1
(MUSIC)

UP →

LAVATORY

DN
UP

STUDIO
NO. 5
(TALKS)

LAV'Y

GREEN
ROOM

UP LIFT DN

Silence
Cabinet

STUDIO NO. 4
(VARIETY)

NORTH WEST BUILDING
2nd Floor

(December – 25) (H1)

UP →

LAV'Y

DN →

GREEN
ROOM

LAVATORY

ECHO
ROOM

UP LIFT DN

UP

Glazed
over

Glass
Doors

EFFECTS ROOM

Glass
Doors

Silence Cabinet/
Mixer Unit

STUDIO NO. 2 (DRAMA)

Observ'n Window

hold a chair and a little table on which the small black box was placed (Gielgud, pp. 22/23). He omitted to mention that the box in fact had four knobs, the third connecting the microphone in the Echo Room and a right-hand knob controlling the producer's own microphone though, until 1927, the mixer could only cope with two sources at any one time.

The Echo Room performed a double function in that it provided direct access via a few steps to the IEE Building. It seems that from 9 a.m. to 6 p.m. it served as a corridor and in the evening as an Echo Room, the connecting door to the IEE block being locked each evening. The small isolated rear room served for a while as a small Green Room for actors and actresses.

Immediately below the Drama Studio/ Effects Room, another specialist studio was created on the first floor. This was the 'Variety Studio' otherwise known as 'No. 4'. It was about 44ft long, 21ft wide and 11ft high (West, p.12) and was designed to create the right ambience for artistes in that it allowed space for a small audience who looked towards a stage lit with amber spotlights. It was equipped with a special cabinet for the producer - a studio within the studio. Abutting Studio - 4 was a 'Green Room', or 'Artistes Waiting Room', which extended rearward, flanking the stairwell. From the rear of this room, a short curving stair gave easy access to Studio - 1 in the IEE block,* enabling the Green Room to serve both studios.

Opposite the door to Studio - 4 was the entrance to the small Talks Studio, Studio - 5. This was used for reading the news which, by means of linking land-lines, was broadcast simultaneously from all stations, the one newsreader being heard throughout Britain. Studio - 5 was also equipped with a gramophone (record player in today's parlance) (A. G. D. West, *Wireless World*, 2 March 1927). This was equipped with two turn-tables and electromagnetic pick-up devices. A switch put these into circuit changing over from one to the other as required. The gramophone was hornless, the electrical energy being taken from the pick-up unit and fed into the studio's 'A' amplifier. There was therefore no sound within the studio itself.

With three studios on the lower floors of the North West Building and more planned in the lower part of the adjoining Mansions, it made good sense to treat the North Entrance as the 'Artistes' Entrance and to provide a welcoming environment for them. Even Studio No. 1 in the IEE building was readily accessible from the North Entrance. No. 3, the original Studio, took a back seat, being little used for either daytime rehearsals or evening perform-ances. Studio - 3 was used mainly for impromptu, low-key morning broadcasts; in the evening one would find the BBC accompanist there waiting by the piano to cover long intervals between programmes or any breakdown in the service.

So, from December 1925, the artiste

* This stair, and the studio itself, was often used illegally as a short cut from one part of the building to another (Ruth Cockerton, writing in the *BBC House Magazine ARIEL*, June 1938).

arriving at No. 2 Savoy Hill would find a box sign, illuminated after dark, showing a hand pointing up the slope towards the Mansions and carrying the words: TO THE STUDIOS - NORTH ENTRANCE. Round the corner was the North Entrance, tall and narrow and bearing its date of construction - 1925. Beyond the inner doors a short flight of steps led up to the lift and main stair. To the left were two waiting rooms, the larger one which looked on to the street was the prestigious 'Drawing Room' for special visitors and artistes. In Corporation years it was presided over by the official host, Colonel Brand, a magnificent figure with his white moustache and genial manner. Special teas, if not stronger drinks, were served in the Drawing Room. The rear room housed the bulk of visitors, press people, relations of performers and artistes overflowing from the Drawing Room. The room was thoughtfully equipped with a public telephone.

To the right of the stair there were again two rooms. According to P. P. Eckersley, who was responsible for premises (before Tudsbery's appointment in January 1926),* The front room was to serve as a Band Room for those taking part in revues such as the popular 'Radio Radiance' which involved a chorus and high kick dance steps; whilst the rear room housed the Outside Messengers - mostly boys of fourteen or fifteen.

Unlike the Inside Messengers who sorted the post and delivered it to office in-trays, the Outside Messengers were available for physical tasks like putting up music stands or filling office inkwells,

spraying against mosquitoes etc. But they also acted as page-boys calling taxis for visitors and artistes and escorting theatrical stars to Savoy Hill. There were about a dozen 'boys' all in blue serge suits and ready, on the instant, to do the House Superintendent's bidding. He had only to stand at his office door on the ground floor and shout 'Boy'.

It is not certain that the front room actually served as a Band Room for 'Radio Radiance' and other musical groups, as it was soon obvious that the three new studios with their flimsy walls were by no means ideal for musical performances. Instead they were devoted largely to the spoken word. As a result, the need for a Band Room may not have been so pressing as the need for a 'Common Room' for announcers. That such a room existed for announcers in 1926 is evident from the Staff Directory which gives its number as '88' suggesting a ground floor location by the North Entrance.

There were two announcers for day-time and two for evening broadcasts and they alternated at weekends. Over them was the Chief Announcer who liaised with the various programme departments and briefed the announcers each day. Grisewood describes the Announcers' Room 'where we kept our papers and logs and where we did any clerical work that was necessary. It was a fair-sized room with a partition which divided it from a smaller room in which we kept our evening clothes: we used this smaller

* Eckersley's proposals are set out in a paper dated end-1925 in the BBC's Written Archives.

room as a changing room'. Provision of this new accommodation at the close of 1925 meant that a new regime could be imposed: under '4 January 1926' Hibberd noted in his diary - 'First day of evening dress for announcers' (Hibberd, p.15: Grisewood, p. 146).

The arrangements for Studios 4 and 5 were by no means ideal. Noise impinged from people entering the hall below, from the lift, and from messenger boys in hobnailed boots running up the stairs. These stairs had brass nosings so the effect was like the clatter of a railway train. One desperate BBC official suggested to Reith that an allowance be given to staff to buy crêpe-soled shoes! Meanwhile these miscellaneous noises must have added a curious background to the daily news reading.

Downstairs in the Basement was the BBC tea-room or buffet. It was available throughout the day and during the evening (L. Chilman, *Wireless World*, 30 March 1927). It was a boon to evening performers as well as to those arriving during the day for auditions or rehearsals. The tea-room also served BBC staff but this internal service probably amounted to little more than beverages, the basement kitchen supplying a staff tea-point on the third (?) floor overlooking the IEE buildings. One bought a supply of tickets at the beginning of the week, a penny ticket covering tea and a bun. This fare could be supplemented with tuppenny bars of Cadbury's chocolate kept by the senior Office Boy in a stationary cupboard.

There was no staff canteen as such.

Older hands among the men would frequent nearby pubs like Mooneys where excellent bread and cheese could be had with a glass of stout. For the younger men there was Harry Fitch's Refreshment Rooms across the road in Savoy Street. For his part 14 year old Jim Herring often got a hot lunch at an Italian Restaurant in Exeter Street the other side of the Strand; but at 10d it must have made quite a hole in his wage packet of 15/-. Other lads like Arthur Miles remember going to a room in Savoy Street to 'eat our sandwiches and drink bottles of pop'; this was presumably at No. 10 where the BBC rented space from October 1926. For their part, senior officials tended to congregate in the Coal Hole tavern just up the passage from Savoy Hill, or perhaps enjoy a business lunch at Rules in Maiden Lane (Gorham, p 24: R.. H. Eckersley, p. 58).

Nevertheless the BBC Tea-Room, under the care of Mrs Hudson, was much in demand and never more so than during the General Strike in May 1926, when it had to provide breakfasts for those staff and policemen sleeping over-night in the building to guard it against the strikers.

General view of the Control Room at 2LO, January, 1927 *(reproduced by permission of the BBC)*

6. ENLARGEMENT OF CONTROL ROOM

The temporary Control Room only served for eighteen months before being overtaken by the growing demands placed on its limited capacity. It now served two transmitters - the new 3kW '2LO' transmitter, built on the roof of Selfridges, and the 25kW '5XX' transmitter constructed on a hill near Daventry to broadcast London programmes across rural England.

The first took over from Marconi House on 6 April 1925 and 5XX Daventry opened on 27 July 1925. The second development was the proliferation in the number of studios: programme departments would, by the end of 1925, have their own specialist studios for talks, variety, drama and music. The dance floors of the Savoy Hotel and Hotel Cecil, and their almost nightly broadcasts, constituted, in effect, additional studios. Thirdly, the SB gear had to be rejigged to cope with eight new relay stations established between May and December

1924 in key cities.* Finally, there was an ever-increasing number of permanent O.B. lines feeding Savoy Hill: the 75 lines of April 1924 had, by November 1925, increased to 200 (West, P.13).

Fortunately, there was space for a larger Control Room as, in the summer of 1925, the Research and Development Workshops, which had flanked the old Control Room, had been moved to the top floor of the Mansions. By demolishing two walls and a corridor ceiling the Control Room could expand absorbing both the southern workshop and the corridor. (A. C. Shaw writing in *World Radio*, 15 November 1935). Part of the northern Workshop became the new

Control Room's Battery Room, the remainder being equipped with a loud-speaker and used as a Listening Room for checking the quality of broadcast transmissions (A. C. Shaw, *Wireless World*, 9 March 1927). The reconstruction had to be squeezed into a matter of hours as far as rewiring was concerned. The heavy lead cable was laid out along the passage, tied up in bundles of a dozen and threaded into new ducts (Pawley).

* Instead of each main station and each relay station being fed by line direct from London, lines connected London to Glasgow (early 1925), Leeds (early 1926) and Gloucester (December 1926). From these three 'Repeater Stations', further lines radiated to link up with the other nearby stations in each area (West, p.15).

Control desk, August, 1927 *(reproduced by permission of the BBC)*

A large model of the new Control Room showing its equipment was placed on public exhibition (For photo of model see *Wireless World*, 9 March 1927).

First, instead of two Control Desks there were now four, a pair of desks being located against each of the side walls. Most of the end wall was taken up with glass-fronted cabinets containing the SB line amplifiers, relay board and fuse panel. In the left hand (south east) corner were positioned the check receivers from 2LO London and 5XX Daventry. In the centre of the room, but close to the SB plant, was placed the SB control desk or 'Switchboard'. Later, in 1926, a line corrector desk for testing and equalising outside broadcast lines was also installed in the centre of the room, the corrector circuits being mounted on the wall between the Control Desks. The wall to the right of the entrance doors carried the master clock and time signal apparatus, and also the switchboard controlling the central battery system installed in the adjoining Battery Room. Here all the amplifier and relay batteries were centralised and a duplicate set of batteries allowed replenishment by the motor generators alongside. Finally each of the long walls carried an illuminated board with numbers representing the studios (initially five): the appropriate number was lit when a studio was 'live', that is, in use for broadcasting.

The general appearance of the room was a contrast to the old tangled mess. Pawley, writing in 1972, captures the atmosphere:

'Expanses of rich mahogany, with highlights of gleaming brass, jostled with exposed coils, valves and heavy wires. Elegant cabinet work and rows of jack-strips reflected the influence of Post Office telephone switchboards. The general effect was of Victorian solidity with, here and there, a touch of the empirical style associated with the name Heath Robinson' (Pawley, p.50).

7. STUDIOS - 6 AND 7 IN MANSIONS

SH-SUMMARY: Entries - 18, 19 (PART), 20 and 22: February 1926/January 1927. No. 1 Studio out of action for re-decorating and Chenil Galleries hired for concerts (February 1926). The whole of Bath Stores (i.e. Savoy Hill Mansions) taken over and notice given to existing tenants on first and second floors (June 1926). Talks Studio (No. 6) completed on first floor of corner wing (summer 1926). No. 7 Studio opened, occupying two floors, and used for Military Band programmes (January 1927).

At the end of Company days the original studio (No. 3) was still in its original 1923 condition and was beginning to attract nostalgic interest (A. G. D. West, *Wireless World*, 16 February 1927). Studio - 1, however, was now the main studio for music output and had to keep abreast of developments in studio technique. In this, Studio - 4 had led the way with the use of variable draping and the introduction of an announcer's cabinet - a studio within a studio. Studio - 1 followed suit a few months later: the old hessian layer was removed and the new lighter curtains were hung on rails so they could be

Studio No. 1 re-modelled and fitted with free-standing Silence Cabinet, March, 1928
(*reproduced by permission of the BBC*)

pulled back to increase reverberation and so provide a richer tone. The Announcer's sound-proof cabinet had windows overlooking the studio and was equipped with its own microphone: red lights showed when it was 'live' as a 'studio' in its own right. One advantage was that the cabinet could be used at rehearsals to check the sound quality and adjust the position of orchestral instruments: another was that the announcer could introduce items on the programme without being disturbed by the orchestra as the instrumentalists entered, tuned up, and received instructions from the conductor. In short, it improved continuity. The opportunity was also taken to incorporate an improved system of studio ventilation, comparable to that in Studios 2, 4 and 5 (*BBC Year Book* 1930, p. 174). The upgrading of Studio - 1 took till after May to complete and during this period the Chenil Galleries in Chelsea were used with a land line linking them to the Control Room at Savoy Hill. The new Studio - 1 provided the largest uncluttered room at Savoy Hill and was used not only for orchestral rehearsals and broadcasts but also for staff meetings.

Sir Walford Davies' transmission to schools, Music Studio (No. 7) January, 1928

Here too, Miss Osborne conducted her physical drill classes following her appointment as a secretary in February 1926. (Ruth Cockerton *op. cit.*).

In June 1926 the remaining floors of the Mansions were taken and by August, Studio - 6 had been completed.

It is not easy to discern the layout of the first and second floors. As a starting point, we need to locate the two new studios. Both were on the first floor but Studio - 7, 43ft by 20ft, was 22ft 6in high, taking up the full height of the first and second floors (Payne, p. 51). Only the central portion of Savoy Hill Mansions

had room for such a large studio where it would have occupied three out of the four bays, the fourth probably serving as a Band Room. A night-time photograph of the Mansions taken at this time shows the six blacked-out windows of Studio - 7 contrasting with the illuminated windows all around. The photograph demonstrates that the studio occupied the three eastern bays of the central portion of the Mansions, the Band Room bay being on the west side. The 'hall-like' proportions of Studio - 7 were inspired by those of the lounge of the Grand Hotel, Eastbourne, from which excellent transmissions of Albert Sandler's orchestra had been relayed in 1925. The 'hall' had a rich brown and gold interior with an organ at one end. It was especially suited to small orchestral combinations such as dance bands and octets. Here the resident BBC dance bands played - Sydney Firman, Jack Payne from 1928 and Henry Hall in April 1932.*

Studio - 6 was intended for talks and for incidental piano transmissions, for instance those music talks given and illustrated by Sir Walford Davies. It was the first to dispense with traditional draping of walls and ceiling, being given the appearance of a comfortable drawing room. The desired acoustics were achieved by using hair felt hidden by wallpaper. Pictures and tapestries were not merely ornamental but actually improved the acoustics. The reference in the *SH-Summary* to the studio's location in 'the corner wing' implies it was in the eastern portion of the Mansions, not in the central portion. Grisewood describes how, as announcer for the evening, he would literally run from the Variety Studio (at the western end) to the No. 6 studio (at the eastern end) to read the news (Grisewood p. 130). Studio - 6 was the largest room in the east wing: it could in fact accommodate the BBC Chorus of 26 singers! (L. Chilman, *Wireless World*, 30 March 1927).

Photographic evidence is helpful in locating the Music Library. This long room also had angled walls and occupied the rear of the central portion of the Mansions. In the care of Frank Hook (from the beginning of the BBC) its first

floor location was shared with the main Music Studios - Nos. 1 and 7 as well as Studio - 4 (Variety).

Room numbers shown in the BBC Directory indicate that the other rooms on the first floor were either unoccupied or occupied by junior staff. But at second floor, space appears to have been largely taken up by engineering directors responsible for Research (West), Land-lines/SB (Attkins), South Area Maintenance (Florence), and Premises/Fixed Equipment (Tudsbery).

At ground level we not only have a plan with room numbers (see Section - 4 above), but most of these rooms are listed in the BBC Staff Directory of 1926. The central portion was largely the preserve of the Head of Drama and Variety (Jeffrey) who now had his own Variety and Drama Studios nearby. Also on the ground floor was the large room used by the leaders of the London Station Orchestra and Chorus (Kneale Kelly and Stanford Robinson) and the first conductor of the 2LO Dance Band (Sydney Firman). By the East Entrance was the BBC bookshop. Here too, ready for a quick get-away, was the OB Engineer (Thompson) with his equipment immediately below in the Basement ready to be loaded into the BBC lorry parked in the little passage alongside. With the

*Studio 7 was the setting of an unusual experiment on 15 October 1931 when Jack Payne's Band not only broadcast, but was televised as it did so, the conductor being bathed in a vivid pale blue light. In the next room, which was darkened, a Baird disc receiver showed a flickering image on a tiny orange screen.

lifting of restrictions on broadcasting running commentaries and eye-witness accounts at the end of 1926, the OB Engineer was going to be very much in demand and Thompson was soon joined by Robert Wood who was to manage many great broadcasts of national events in the ensuing three decades.

Drama Studio Effects Room in Mansions basement, June, 1930
(reproduced by permission of the BBC)

8.   STUDIOS IN BASEMENT OF MANSIONS

SH-SUMMARY: Entries - 19 (PART), 24 and 28: June 1926/May 1928. Control Board approval given for building two new studios in Bath Buildings basement (June 1926). New dramatic studio in basement of east wing (old Bath Stores) came into use, with effects room and echo room, numbered No. 2. Old No. 2 Studio was numbered No. 8 (May 1927) and remodelled (May 1928). No. 9 Studio opened in Basement of east wing, used chiefly for Chamber Music (May 1928).

Leaving aside the North West Building, the Mansions was permanently occupied from the top downwards in three stages - the Fifth, Fourth and Third Floors in June 1925; the Second, First and Ground Floors in 1926; and the Basement in 1927/28. In this account we are concerned primarily with the 'Company' years but it is relevant to show how the BBC's occupation of the Mansions was completed.

The plan itself survives in the IEE archives, under the title 'Proposed Alterations to Basement for the British Broadcasting Co. Ltd': it is signed by Tudsbery, BBC Director of Premises, and is dated 1926. Under the plan, the stair up to the East Entrance was retained and so too was another leading up from the Central Stores at the end of the building into Savoy Street. The corridor was however offset to leave a wider rear expanse in which to place the new studios. The drama studio suite occupied the whole of the central portion of the Mansions Basement with the Chamber Music Studio in the eastern portion. The plan shows two new Echo Rooms remote from any studio.

The arrangements for drama production were almost identical to those on the second floor of the North West Building namely a square drama studio with a square Effects Room on one side and an Echo Room on the other. The Effects Room, as before, included a producer's Silence Room with a window looking into the main studio and this was flanked by glass doors separating the studio from the Effects Room. The sizes of the three rooms reflected those on the second floor and the new studio was even given the same number - 'Studio - 2'. The old Studio - 2 was thereupon closed for remodelling and enlargement.

The two new Echo Rooms on the Basement's street frontage were for 'Artificial Echo'. They did not receive sound from an adjoining room but could be linked electrically to any studio which required an echo enrichment to its speech or music. The studio needing this facility was equipped with a double-decker 'meat-safe' containing two microphones 'A' and 'B' the latter linked to the Artificial Echo Room where, by means of an echo amplifier, the signal operated a loudspeaker. The loud-speaker's reverberant sound was picked up by microphone 'C' installed in the Echo Room. Microphones 'A' and 'C' were linked to an echo control mixer in the Control Room. The mixer meant that different degrees of echo could be obtained: just by turning a knob, the control engineer could convert the rather dead sound from a heavily draped studio into a resonant sound or even a full cathedral effect (A. G. D West, *Wireless World*, 23 February 1927).

If a Control Engineer could mix sounds from any distant studio and any remote Echo Room so too could the producer of a play. A new type of dramatic control panel capable of linking up with any studio, Effects Room or Echo Room, and with any combination of these at any one time, was developed during 1927 and perfected by May 1928. It was a far cry from the little black box which mixed the local sounds in the old Studio - 2 suite on the second floor. The 'Panel' with its long row of control knobs, its cue-light switches, its 'talk-back' key and microphone for the producer's use, had taken on something of the size and shape of an organ key-board and rated a room of its own for its accommodation (Gielgud, p.24). This room was itself

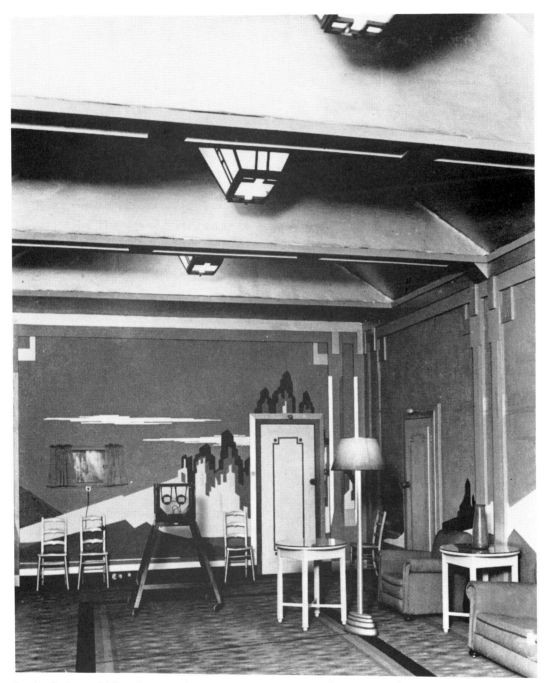

Studio 3, Savoy Hill with microphone stand and 2 Marconi Reisz microphones

(reproduced by permission of the BBC)

Dramatic control panel, Room 97, Savoy Hill Mansions, May, 1928 *(reproduced by permission of the BBC)*

remote from any studio, echo or effects room: it was Room 97, forming part of the Dramatic Productions offices on the ground floor of the Mansions (*BBC Handbook* for 1928, p.162).*

With the Basement Drama Studio in operation from May 1927, the way was clear to reconstruct the old drama studio and Effects Room as a single large drama studio. This was ready by May 1928 and was re-numbered 'Studio - 8'. Studio - 8 could of course, now make use of the Basement Effects Room equipment as well as incidental music or crowd effects from other studios; and each of these could be augmented by using one or more of the four echo rooms. Without doubt, these technical advances in accommodation and equipment did much

to advance the art of radio drama in the last years of Savoy Hill under the imaginative guidance of Val Gielgud, Lance Sieveking, Cecil Lewis and others.

Studio - 9 in the eastern portion of the Basement was built for Chamber Music and had its own Silence Room for the announcer, its window looking into the studio. Like all the Basement rooms, it used solid sound-proof walls and, like the new Studio - 2, was entered via a sound-proof vestibule. The Basement studios were undraped: they used

* A description of the original Dramatic Control Panel is given in the *Radio Times* for 15 June 1928 under the title 'How a Radio Play is Mixed'. This article was the fifth in the series 'Savoy Hill with the Lid Off'. A technical description is given in *The Stuff of Radio* (Sieveking, p. 397).

absorbent wall linings stuck direct to the brick walls and finished with a decorative wallpaper, in short, the acoustic treatment adopted for Studios - 6 and 7. Studio - 9's opening in May 1928 enabled Studio - 3 to be taken out of service and divested of its multiple layers of hessian in favour of the new acoustic treatment. As a result by 1929 Savoy Hill had four specialised music studios (nos.1, 3, 7 and 9), three drama/variety studios (nos. 2, 4 and 8), and two Talks studios (nos. 5 and 6), all built or remodelled within a period of little more than three years.

Savoy Hill had become technically sophisticated, the physical developments being complemented by advances in broadcasting technique and equipment, advances whose evolution during the early 'twenties is described in the next Chapter.

(reproduced by permission of the BBC)

Chamber Music Studio (No. 9), Basement, Savoy Hill Mansions, May, 1928

STUDIO DESIGN AND EQUIPMENT FOR BROADCASTING

I. STUDIOS: ACOUSTIC TREATMENT

In July 1922, following advice from the director of a gramophone company, the 2LO studio at Marconi House was draped with thin white muslin in an attempt to smother the slightest echo and so simplify the task of the microphone. This muslin soon became dingy in the sooty London air. Peter Eckersley writing in *Popular Wireless* in late 1925 described it as 'dirty mosquito netting'. (West, p.5).

The struggle to eliminate echo was enormously intensified when the first studio at Savoy Hill came to be constructed in April 1923. No less than five layers of canvas, with one inch gaps between them, were stretched on wooden frameworks over virtually the whole of the walls and ceiling. A sixth layer comprised yellow net curtains, again over walls and ceiling. The floor was covered in a thick blue carpet. This treatment brought the reverberation time down to a quarter of a second. On the other hand, the extreme deadness imposed a severe strain on the artistes. But, with its freedom from standing-wave effects,* the studio proved an ideal testing ground for microphones (West, pp. 11/12).

The normal appropriate reverberation time varies from 0.75 second for speech to 1 second for a singer or 1½ for an octet; a large orchestra might require two, or even four, seconds.

Experimental microphone used at Marconi House, early 1923

There was therefore no reason for reducing a studio's reverberation below 0.7 second once the microphone's experimental phase was successfully completed. Accordingly the first floor studio of 1924 was given only a single layer of hessian, this being concealed behind draped curtains. The studio was particularly good for orchestral works, but not ideal.

The problem was that the reverberation time was not only too

* Sound strengths arising from reflected sounds may be additive or subtractive. The result is known as the 'Standing Wave Effect'.

Marconi-Sykes Magnetophone, 1924

(reproduced by permission of the Marconi Company, Ltd.)

short but, more importantly, that it varied across the frequency range giving prominence to low frequencies at the expense of high ones. The former enjoyed over a second reverberation while the latter enjoyed less than half a second. There was therefore a lack of brilliance in the studio's output of music. Even so, Studio - I was a great improvement on the original third floor studio where the higher frequencies were well nigh eliminated.

In February 1926 the Studio was remodelled, orchestras being temporarily transferred to the Chenil Galleries in Chelsea as no other Savoy Hill studio was suitable. First, the hessian lining was removed, increasing the reverberation time from 0.7 to 0.9 second; secondly, the curtain covering was hung on rollers so that it could be drawn aside, allowing the reverberation to be increased up to a maximum of 1.3 seconds (A. G. D. West, *Wireless World*, 16 February 1927).

The studios built in the North West Building towards the end of 1925 had thin internal walls which were liable to 'rattle'. It was decided to use them primarily for speech rather than for music: Studio - 2 was used for drama, Studio - 4 for Variety and Studio - 5 for news and talks. The draping of Studio - 4 could be pulled aside for this studio was not limited to the spoken word: singers performed as well as other artistes. Studio - 2 was used for drama and had fixed draping but the adjoining Effects Room had variable draping. Studio - 5 was permanently draped with a fairly thick casement cloth. The studio still exhibited a very strong boom effect due to the light construction of one of its walls. This wall was therefore covered with a one inch layer of hair felt underneath the decorative draping.

Studio design changed about the middle of 1926 from draped walls to sound absorbent wall linings. Studio - 6 used ½ inch thick hair felt with strong wallpaper. This reduced reverberation to 0.8 second and yet enabled the walls to have the appearance of a traditional drawing room. Half the ceiling had a felt lining, the other half being left bare to add reflection so the speaker could hear himself talking. The wallpaper alone was not entirely satisfactory as it created high-toned reflection or 'chink'. The effect was minimised by hanging pictures and tapestries on the walls to scatter any reflected sound (*Wireless World*, 16 February 1927).

For music large studios were essential to ensure good reverberation and, to obtain the required volume, Studio - 7 was built double-height. The floor was covered in a layer of Celotex, an under-felt and thick carpet. The walls had wooden ventilation ducts running horizontally and wooden pillars. The panels between were covered in felt and wallpaper. The ceiling was hung with heavy draping which could be pulled aside to increase the reverberation from 0.8 to 1.6 seconds (A. G. D. West, *Wireless World*, 23 February 1927). Used by dance bands and military bands, Studio - 7 was the last to be built in Company days.

Felt linings were ideal for eliminating the earlier problem of dominant low frequencies and wallpaper provided an attractive decor. Accordingly this solution was also used for the Basement Studios, the last to be built at Savoy Hill. But wallpaper, especially when painted, could lead to dominant high frequencies ('chink'). The answer was to re-introduce light curtains hanging in loose folds over at least part of the studio. It appears this solution was employed in the 1928 reconstruction of the upper Drama Studio (*BBC Year Book* 1931, pp. 288/289).

It is clear that most studios were limited to less than a second of reverberation, not enough to create special effects like those of a hall or cathedral. To obtain a richer, fuller sound for broadcasting, the concept of artificial echo was introduced. The upper Drama Studio was the first to have this facility. It took the form of an Echo Room leading off from the studio. Sound reaching this room through the open door was picked up on the Echo Room microphone. The producer was equipped with a control panel which enabled him to select from either microphone, or to mix the sounds in any desired proportion. In other words he could select any reverberation level he chose and was thereby able to create a sense of location - a small room, a large room, a hall, a church or a cathedral with a full 4-second reverberation time.

In theory the same arrangement could be applied to the music studios, numbers 1, 3 and 7. But the building layout prevented this. The solution was to provide an Echo Room remote from the studio. The studio was either equipped with a second microphone or its microphone amplifier was modified to create a second circuit. Either way, the second line led to the Echo Room where the signal was amplified so as to work a loudspeaker. The sounds from this reverberated round the bare walls and were picked up by the Echo Room's microphone. Signals from the Echo Room microphone and from the Studio microphone could then be blended in any proportion in the Control Room.

The concept of a remote Echo Room was tested in 1926 using the Drama Studio's Echo Room; similar experiments were carried out in corridors and also using Studio - 7 when under construction and in its bare state. Two 'remote' Echo Rooms were then constructed in the Basement of the Mansions.

2. MICROPHONES, AMPLIFIERS AND CONTROL DESKS

The microphone and amplifier in use at Marconi House in early 1923 had a 'Jurassic Age' character; both were big and heavily constructed. The microphone's diaphragm had a pronounced resonance so several microphones, each tuned to a different resonance, were used together. Four of these massive instruments, each weighing twenty pounds, were mounted in a wooden box which was set on a tripod stand. The box could be raised or lowered by means of a gear wheel. This microphone, known as the 'Electrodynamic' or 'Round' microphone (after its Marconi inventor) needed an amplifier. This too was of gigantic size - 8ft long, 2ft deep and 4ft 6in high.* It needed a room to itself, not only because of its size, but because it was temperamental reacting violently to the least disturbance (A. C. Shaw writing in World Radio, 15 November 1935).

Unlike the microphone, the amplifier was moved to Savoy Hill where it served the original studio. It was located in the 'Instrument Room' or 'Workshop'. Although in the North Wing, this adjoined the Studio Suite. The amplifier was divided into six metal compartments, three above and three below. The former held the valves and various components, while the latter held the L.T. and H.T.

supplies. There were six stages of amplification, the number of valves used being ten. The last stage consisted of four valves in parallel. These were bright emitters and gave such a strong glare it was necessary to cover them up. The first stages in this amplifier were extremely sensitive and responded to mechanical vibrations even better than to electrical impulses. All the 'tricks of the trade' were tried to suppress the 'ponging' which resulted. For example, the valves were suspended in mid-air by springs covered in cotton wool. Another 'trick' was to suspend the valves upside-down in beakers of thick oil. Once the equipment was ready for work one dared not move any wires or even approach too near. 'Many grey hairs were brought to the heads of the engineers owing to the announcer 'ponging' the amplifier when hurrying from the studio to the amplifier room to learn whether all was well' (A. C. Shaw writing in World Radio, 15 November 1935).

With the opening of the first Savoy Hill studio, a new microphone appeared on the old tripod. It looked very unstable with its box perched on a cushion of sorbo rubber on the tiny triangular shelf of the stand. It was also very experimental but it was the prototype of the microphone that was to become in 1924 the standard BBC type and almost the symbol of broadcasting in the company years and beyond. The

* The dimensions given by West are incorrect as height and width have been transposed. Harold Bishop later gave the length as 6ft, height 4ft, depth 2ft (BBC Year Book 1948, p.23).

January, 1927

Marconi GA1 or `A' amplifier for magnetophone
Marconi GK1 or `B' amplifier

Control position No. 2 with a Jackfield unit and a `B' amplifier *(reproduced by permission of the BBC)*

microphone was known as the 'Marconi-Sykes Magnetophone'. It consisted of a pot-shaped iron container with a central pole. Polarising winding round the pole produced an intense magnetic field in the air gaps between the pole and the outer casing. A coil of aluminium wire shaped like a disc was lightly mounted at the open end of the pot on tufts of cotton wool and vaseline, these being bedded against a circular felt pad. The sound waves impinging on this coil caused it to vibrate, thus generating an E.M.F. in the coil due to the latter cutting the lines of force across the gap. To prevent any vibration being communicated except by way of the coil diaphragm, the heavy microphone was laid in a sling of spongy rubber, this being supported in a frame. The frame usually had a cover of copper gauze and silk to prevent the moving diaphragm being damaged by careless handling or by air currents set up by the studio's ventilating fans. On one of the legs of the stand was a knife-switch for the magnetising supply.

Soon the magnetophone was supported on a purpose-made four legged mahogany pedestal mounted on wheels to enable it to be moved about the studio. With the advent of new amplifiers in April 1924 the old sharp clicks in the headphones as the knife switch was employed between artistes' performances became a thing of the past. Instead the energising current was gradually reduced and an effect was obtained similar to the fading out of a picture on a cinema screen (Burrows, pp. 96/97).

The new amplifiers of April 1924 in effect completed the Marconi system for broadcasting, that is, the Magnetophone, the microphone amplifier, the control amplifier and the 1.5 kW 'Q' transmitter which had been developed from the Marconi House prototype of 1922.* During 1924 virtually all the BBC stations were fitted with this Marconi equipment though Birmingham remained a notable exception. At Savoy Hill, it was now possible to position the control (or 'B') amplifiers remote from the studios and to make the one amplifier available to more than one studio. This gave rise to two key concepts; first the grouping of technical equipment in a 'Control Room' and secondly the creation of a Control Desk housing the 'B' amplifier flanked by input and output boards to allow routing of material from any source and to any desired destination.

The Control Desk operator, though remote from the studio, could keep in touch by means of bell push phone and indicator lights. Burrows describes how the engineers would signal to the studio that all was ready by arranging for red lamps over the studio doors to flicker. The producer signalled back that he was ready by pressing the bell push. The engineers in the Control Room would then connect the studio to the transmitter and switch the red lights on permanently to indicate that the studio was 'live'. (Burrows, p. 91). Later, the Control Room was fitted with a wall-mounted panel showing duplicated numbers representing the individual studios - initially five, later seven and finally, in 1928, nine). When the announcer or producer 'buzzed' the Control Desk the source of the buzz showed up as a green figure illuminated at the bottom of the panel. When the engineer made the studio 'live' the corresponding red figure above was illuminated on the panel in place of the green figure. A double buzz from the studio indicated the programme was over and that the studio should be taken off the aerial: it activated the green number on the board. The control engineer would immediately fade down his controls and switch off both the studio's red light and the red number on his board. (*Radio Times*, 20 April 1928).

In the first Control Room of April 1924, the Control Desk was duplicated. This allowed smoother, speedier transitions to or from SB to occur and likewise to or from OBs and from one

* The Marconi system was described in a contemporary Company booklet under the title *The Art and Technique of Broadcasting*, issued in 1924. A description of the magnetophone and its 'A' and 'B' amplifiers was also given by H.J. Round in *Wireless World*, 26 November 1924.

London studio to another. With the increase in the number of studios at the end of 1925 the Control Room was extended to allow for four Control Desks as well as for the growing size of the SB equipment.

At the end of 1925 the new Marconi-Reisz microphone made its bow at Savoy Hill. It was more compact and robust, and therefore easy to handle. Its output was far greater than the Magnetophone's and it had a more even frequency response. The Marconi-Reisz microphone comprised a block of marble with channels cut in it and filled with carbon dust in which the electrodes were embedded. The carbon dust was kept in place by a thin mica diaphragm. To begin with the microphone was housed in the old 'meat-safe' usually in pairs. In 1926, a double decker version of the meat-safe appeared but before long the microphones were being suspended from the ceiling or from stands. The reason for having two microphones was to enable one to be available for connecting up to the Echo Room whenever artificial echo was required (West, p. 18 and A. G. D. West, *Wireless World*, 2 March 1927). By the close of Company days, the Marconi-Reisz microphone had virtually swept the board.§ Its greater sensitivity made it unnecessary any longer for the 'A' amplifiers to be located in, or close to, the studio and, early in 1927, they were replaced by amplifiers of BBC design concentrated in a room on the first floor of the Mansions (West, p.14).

§ The Marconi-Reisz microphone was not, however, unchallenged. In 1929 one of the Savoy Hill studios was equipped with a Western Electric condenser microphone and, by the end of Savoy Hill days, the condenser microphone was to be found in all the more important studios before making its début at Broadcasting House in its improved 'slack diaphragm' form.

Marconi-Reisz microphone, 1926
(reproduced by permission of the Marconi Company, Ltd.)

3. SB EQUIPMENT LINKING ALL STATIONS

Perhaps the biggest broadcasting event marking the start of the BBC was the series of opera broadcasts from Covent Garden. This Outside Broadcast (OB) successfully made use of a land-line provided by the GPO. It occurred to the BBC's new Chief Engineer that if Covent Garden could be relayed and broadcast by 2LO, perhaps the BBC's Birmingham Studio could be relayed and broadcast by 2LO - and vice versa. And if 2LO could be relayed by land-line and broadcast by Birmingham, it could surely at the same time be relayed by other land-lines to other BBC stations and broadcast - in short we would have simultaneous broadcasting (S.B.). This could offer economies; but more important, it would mean that major events could be broadcast across the nation. One such event, shortly to occur, would be King George V's opening of the British Empire Exhibition at Wembley on 23 April 1924. This would constitute both an OB and an SB.

Following land-line tests in March and April, the first experimental SB broadcasts occurred on 13 May 1923 from Marconi House using a Western Electric 40 watt amplifier and speech input equipment. These were placed in a small room close to the transmitter, this room thereby serving as the distribution centre with PO lines to the five other BBC stations (Newcastle, Cardiff, Glasgow, Manchester, Birmingham). The 'studio' on this occasion was an adjoining undraped room equipped with a Western Electric

double-button microphone. Speech was almost unintelligible due to reverberation in the room. More seriously, the high power amplifier caused severe disruption in the telephone trunk line traffic. So in its place, each of the outgoing lines was equipped with a separate amplifier of low power, further amplification being organised at the receiving end. The Savoy Hill studio was used, both speech and music on this occasion (17 May) being broadcast. On 30 May, OB and SB were combined with the final act of 'Hansel and Gretel' being broadcast from all stations, the source being Covent Garden Opera House (E. K. Sandeman, *Wireless World*,

S B amplifier cabinet, January, 1927

(reproduced by permission of the BBC)

First S B board at Savoy Hill, 1923 (*reproduced by permission of the Marconi Company, Ltd.*)

21 May 1924 and C. C. J. Frost, *Wireless World*, 30 June 1923).

After this the SB board with its distinctive bank of Western Electric amplifiers was transferred to Savoy Hill and fitted in a cul-de-sac well away from the Amplifier Room (A. C. Shaw writing in *World Radio*, 15 November 1935). It was located in the only other 3rd floor workshop available - the South Room, West Wing, then in the process of being sub-divided. By 29 August 1923 all was ready and the news from 2LO was from that day forth broadcast simultaneously from all BBC stations. Henceforth only

items of local interest had to be 'phoned through to the various stations - a long and arduous task had been eliminated (Burrows, p.91). The SB Room, strictly a railed off portion of the Development Section's Workshop, became quite famous. It epitomised the new power and influence of radio; one man's voice could be heard simultaneously broadcast from stations hundreds of miles apart.

With the creation of the Control Room in April 1924 the SB Board was transferred and extended to serve the increasing number of main and relay stations. Again it employed Western

Electric amplifiers each with its repeating coil and potentiometer for impedance matching (West, pp.14/15).

As a result of the enlargement of the Control Room in November 1925, the SB rig was yet again moved and streamlined. Thirty 'two-stage' line amplifiers were ranged along the far wall of the Control Room in glass-fronted cabinets. In front of the cabinets was the SB desk from which the system was operated. The Board soon had lines to 5XX Daventry, to the Repeater Stations at Leeds, Glasgow and Gloucester and to the main station at Bournemouth and the Nottingham Relay Station. The line amplifiers gave the programme sufficient strength for its journey and lamps on the Board showed that all was well. There were keys for listening and keys for testing (*Radio Times*, 20 April 1928). The installation was extremely versatile and many of the operations were carried out automatically so one engineer could easily control it. (West, p.16). In 1926 a line corrector desk for transmission measurements and equalisation was added, the corrector circuits being mounted on the west wall between the Control Desks. The purpose of these was to ensure that all musical frequencies were transmitted with equal amplitude. This, in effect, converted telephone lines designed for speech into lines that could faithfully convey music.

Savoy Hill control room, May, 1932

74

4. QUALITY CONTROL

Throughout the Company years music made up a very large proportion of broadcast output: around three-fifths of an average day in November 1923; almost two-thirds in 1926 though the increase was largely in the popular field (Kenyon, p. 7). Throughout the period the placing of artistes and instrumentalists relative to the microphone and to each other was a major pre-occupation. The Marconi booklet, *The Art and Technique of Broadcasting* (published early in 1924), included a plan showing the ideal positioning for members of a wireless

2LO and 5XX check receivers in Control Room, April, 1928 (*reproduced by permission of the BBC*)

orchestra in a studio. Significantly the plan shows a mere 13 players. A later plan of 1927 shows the distribution of the London Wireless Orchestra and chorus. It shows 33 instrumentalists and 26 singers (H. L. Chilman, *Wireless World*, 30 March 1927).* Throughout the period the positioning of artistes and members of the orchestra was done by experiment. An engineer wearing headphones would sit in a soundproof cubicle and give directions through a small glass window on the basis of the sounds he heard and his judgement as to their musical quality. The original studio (Studio - 3) had an operator's room for this purpose and Studio - 1 used a telephone cabinet placed within the studio.

The first properly designed and equipped cubicle or 'silence cabinet' was that built in Studio - 4 at the end of 1925. It was a wooden kiosk about 6ft by 4ft and glazed round the upper part. As such it was a studio within a studio equipped with its own microphone and red lights - actually neon letter lamps, 'A' for 'Announcer' and 'S' for studio. According to which microphone was in circuit, the appropriate letter lit up. The switch control was within the cabinet, along with a telephone enabling the Announcer to speak to the Control Room during the

* Studio - 1, the largest of the Savoy Hill studios, was not adequate, on acoustical grounds, for an orchestra of more than 35 players. With the formation of the BBC Symphony Orchestra, in late 1930, Savoy Hill became hopelessly inadequate. The BBC accordingly converted a disused warehouse at the south-east end of Waterloo Bridge. This became known as 'Studio 10'.

programme, or for the Control Room to phone the Announcer in which case a bright light shone in the cubicle. As before, the Announcer, or programme producer, would listen on headphones and decide the best disposition of artistes etc. But he could also make announcements whilst artistes changed over, or the piano was moved, without having to worry about incidental noise being broadcast.

Announcers were apparently enthusiastic about having their own inner sanctum. They felt self-conscious making serious announcements in front of forty or fifty people whose one thought was to get out of the hot studio after their work was done. Equally embarrassing were remarks by the announcer over the air about some famous celebrity when that person was himself, or herself, by the microphone. Lewis, in making these points, went on to request cabinets three times the size of the minute telephone boxes used in the past which had been used mainly for checking positioning of performers. He went on to say that he had often given talks from the little room at the end of Studio - 3 and found this satisfactory.

Cabinets similar to that in the Variety Studio (No. 4) were built in the reconstructed Studio - I and probably also in Studio - 7. The original Drama Studio (No. 2) also had a silence cabinet. But they were not ideal. Being light in construction they were not soundproof and had poor internal acoustics. By the end of 1926 it was realised that Silence Cabinets needed to be solidly built next to, but outside, the studio with just one small window. The two Basement studios were designed in this way; also Studio - 8, the large Drama Studio.

During the broadcast the Announcer's job was to announce: not to vet the quality of the music. To deal with quality control a small listening room was created close to the Control Room and fitted with a loudspeaker operating from the check receivers in the Control Room (that is 2LO London or 5XX Daventry). In this room an engineer sat through the whole evening's programme checking the quality of the transmission and ready to contact the relevant studio or the Control Room if quality was unsatisfactory. In this he was assisted by a musician if the programme was of a musical nature (A. C. Shaw, *Wireless World*, 9 March 1927).

Before long, the Listening Room became equipped with its own Music Control Panel reflecting the parallel development of the Dramatic Control Panel. It was also decided that the Listening Room should replicate the normal home environment. Accordingly, a room with a fireplace, armchair, settee, pictures, bookcase and, of course, loud speaker was created at Savoy Hill and fitted with the Music Control Panel. The room chosen for this purpose was Room - 24 off the North Corridor of the IEE building. This already had a fireplace and was of brick construction so it was ready-made for the purpose. But as far as the Company years are concerned, Room - 24 and its Music Control Panel still lay in the future.

Tubular bells used as a time signal, 1923 *(reproduced by permission of the Marconi Company, Ltd.)*

5. TIME-KEEPING, BIG BEN AND THE 'PIPS'

The chiming of Big Ben has been a feature of British broadcasting from its beginning in November 1922. In the earliest days at Marconi House the Westminster chimes were replicated by the Announcer on a set of tubular bells kept in the studio for the purpose.* On the wall close to the tubular bells was an electric clock. It is not clear whether this was ever checked for accuracy but Marconi House was near enough to Big Ben for the sound of the real chimes to be heard by simply opening one of the 7th floor studio's two windows.

With the move from Marconi House to Savoy Hill a new and much more serious attitude towards time-keeping and the broadcast time signal began to be taken. Within a few days a new BBC drill

* In its first weeks, the BBC had a rival, a tiny Marconi station at Writtle, near Chelmsford, Essex, where Tuesday evening broadcasts mainly by Marconi engineers had been going out since February 1922. 2MT ('Two Emma Toc') Writtle, parodied 2LO's time signal, the Writtle 'gongs' being played on milk and ginger beer bottles.

Clock used in studios, 1923/4
(reproduced by permission of Wireless Press)

At thirty seconds before the hour the announcer was to start counting from thirty to fifty-nine guided by the swing of the clock's pendulum. On the sixtieth second the tubular bell would be struck the number of times corresponding to the hour.

The little oration preceding the count was not a nightly performance but was given on every third day.

Clearly, the high blown reference to 'British Broadcasting Standard Time' needed a surer basis than a casual glance towards the studio clock. That clock had to be reliable; and it had to be regularly checked against an unimpeachable source. It was also important that clocks in the Amplifier Room, the SB Room, the Artistes' Waiting Rooms, the Station Director's Room, the Announcer's Room, the Board Room etc, should all agree with one another. The answer was to have a 'master' clock with 'slave' clocks operated by electric impulse. Two such systems were available, both of very high quality. First, the Hope-Jones 'Synchronome' which was installed at Savoy Hill and also in the Cardiff, Newcastle and Glasgow Stations; and secondly Gent's 'Pulsynetic' system. The latter was accurate to one second a week and was installed in the Birmingham Station for nothing, though with a condition that the maker's name was to be mentioned and that lectures by Gent's staff should be broadcast. Those BBC Stations which opened in the second half of 1923 all had

was introduced applicable to all stations. The Announcer was to take up his position one minute before the hour at which the evening programme was to commence and observe the studio clock with these words:

'Stand by for the time signal. This is the British Broadcasting Company's Standard Time. It is guaranteed to be accurate to Greenwich Mean Time▸ within plus or minus five seconds and is probably more accurate than that'.

▸In the summer months the reference to 'Greenwich Mean Time' was replaced with a reference to 'British Standard Time'.

Pulsynetic systems (they were the new permanent stations at Manchester and Birmingham along with those at Bournemouth and Aberdeen). Later, in January 1924, the new Studio - 1 was equipped with a Synchronome regulator identical to that in the earlier Studio - 3. The clock had three dials, a large one for the 'second' hand and two small ones superimposed one above the other for the 'minute' and 'hour' hands respectively. Below was a glass front through which the pendulum could be observed.

The unimpeachable source against which the clocks were checked was the time signal from the Eiffel Tower, Paris, broadcast by telegraphic signal at 10.45 each morning. This was not convenient for making checks during the day so, in June 1923, the BBC arranged for an hourly signal to be provided by the Standard Time Company. Despite all these precautions, it was quite usual for the studio signals to be as much as three or four seconds fast or slow when compared with GMT. One contributing factor was hesitation on the part of some announcers to strike the bell at the exact minute. But by the end of 1923, the 'BBC Standard Time' had achieved an accuracy of about one second (W. G. W. Mitchell: *Time and Weather Signals: The Wireless Annual for Amateurs and Experimenters*: 1924).

Good though this undoubtedly was, the real answer was to directly link GMT, the ultimate time source, to the broadcast signal - no more counting: no more hammering on tubular bells! Frank Hope-Jones, an authority on electric clocks and a leading figure in the Radio Society of Great Britain, suggested that a permanent service of accurate time-pips, one per second, starting from five seconds to the hour and ending on the hour, should be provided directly from the Royal Observatory at Greenwich to the broadcasting studio at Savoy Hill. This was implemented by connecting two highly accurate, if rather vintage, 1874 Dent chronometers at the Observatory to the BBC Control Room. The GMT time-signal and its preceding 'pips' were broadcast regularly from 5 February 1924. (At this stage, the Control Room was itself in the process of formation).

But the old idea of introducing the evening programme with the sound of the Westminster chimes had not been forgotten. Only this time, listeners would hear the actual chimes. 1923 had been introduced on tubular bells; 1924 would be welcomed with Big Ben itself, a microphone being placed on a roof opposite the Houses of Parliament. But for the regular service, the microphone (the magnetophone) was suspended inside the tower having first been bound up in cotton wool and encased in a sealed rubber football bladder to lessen the effect of atmospheric conditions. A land-line connected Big Ben with Savoy Hill and the microphone in the tower was activated by remote control from the Control Room at Savoy Hill (A. C. Shaw, *Wireless World*, 9 March 1927).

So, from March 1924, there was a new drill for the Studio Announcer. At half a minute to seven he would put on his headphones and hear a shrill buzzing sound. This was purposefully radiated by Savoy Hill for two minutes to enable valve users to adjust their sets to the most sensitive positions. Suddenly the chimes of Westminster would come in, followed by the deep, sonorous and slightly harsh note of Big Ben. As the seventh blow is struck the Announcer returns the headphones to their rest and looks towards the entrance door where a red lamp flickers. He presses the bell-push to alert the Control Room that he is ready to go on air. He returns to the microphone and, seeing the red light glowing steadily he starts off with the well-known formula:

'London calling the British Isles. This is the first news bulletin, copyright from Reuter, Press Association, Exchange Telegraph Company, and Central News'. (Burrows, pp.90/91).

It may well be that listeners heard, not just the news, but the studio clock ticking happily in the background! It has been suggested that this was indeed a feature of the early days of broadcasting. By the end of the Company years, a new master clock had been installeded on the north wall of the Control Room beside the apparatus for the Greenwich Time Signal and that for the reception of Big Ben. In the studios 'slave' clocks, encased in soundproof, glazed, square boxes became standard fittings.

The Savoy Hill master clock survived the move to Broadcasting House and continued in service to the mid-sixties. It was then given a humbler role which it dutifully performed until it was finally pensioned off in 1978. Its days would then have been numbered but for its chance recognition as a historic artefact by a BBC engineer with a keen interest in clocks and time keeping. The engineer, Mr Geoffrey Goodship, now retired, is actively restoring the Savoy Hill clock with meticulous care.

A 'twenties set of BBC tubular bells in their grey painted frame also appear to have survived. They were spotted by the author at a school in Surrey. On the top of the frame an inscription reads 'BBC 26R'. The latter may refer to Room - 26 where 2LO's Musicians had their office from September 1923 to mid-1925.

Master Clock, Greenwich Time Signal and tuning note apparatus, May, 1927

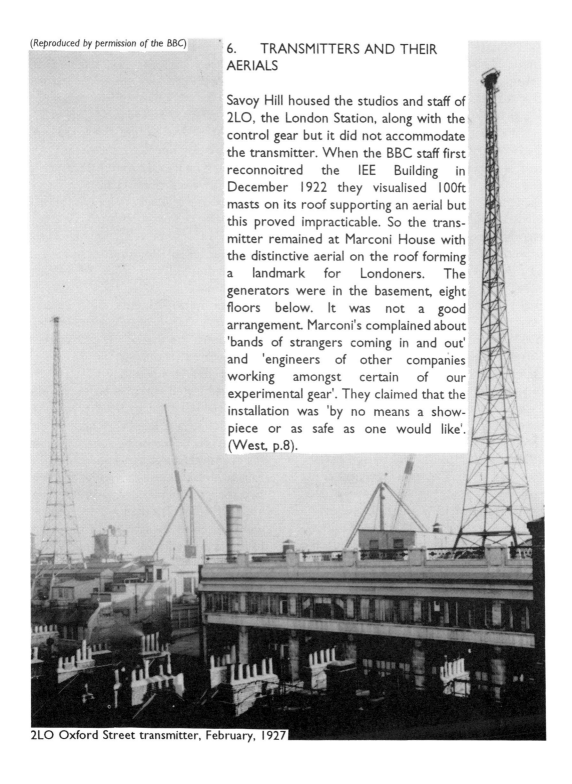

6. TRANSMITTERS AND THEIR AERIALS

Savoy Hill housed the studios and staff of 2LO, the London Station, along with the control gear but it did not accommodate the transmitter. When the BBC staff first reconnoitred the IEE Building in December 1922 they visualised 100ft masts on its roof supporting an aerial but this proved impracticable. So the transmitter remained at Marconi House with the distinctive aerial on the roof forming a landmark for Londoners. The generators were in the basement, eight floors below. It was not a good arrangement. Marconi's complained about 'bands of strangers coming in and out' and 'engineers of other companies working amongst certain of our experimental gear'. They claimed that the installation was 'by no means a showpiece or as safe as one would like'. (West, p.8).

2LO Oxford Street transmitter, February, 1927

Other sites north of the Thames but within a mile or so of Savoy Hill were considered. They had to be well clear of the Admiralty transmitter in Whitehall and that of the Air Ministry in Kingsway. In the end the roof of Selfridges Department Store in Oxford Street was selected. Here huts were erected to house the new transmitter and power plant and two steel pylons 125ft high carried the aerial.* The station used a Marconi double Q transmitter twice as powerful as its predecessor. Its opening, on 6 April 1925, extended the area over which 2LO could be received on crystal sets to about twenty miles radius. But even those with valve sets could only obtain reliable reception if they lived in Surrey, Middlesex or Hertfordshire or, of course, London. Only those tiny portions of Kent, Berkshire, Buckinghamshire and Essex closest to London could be sure of picking up 2LO. This was the position throughout the 'twenties. Meanwhile from 1925 the old Marconi House transmitter (see figs. 3 and 4) was retained as a stand-by.

In October 1929, 2LO closed down in favour of the new London Regional Station at Brookmans Park in Hertfordshire. The little old Marconi House set was installed in the new station as a primitive museum piece from another era. After the war, it was discovered still at Brookmans Park but in a large shed containing some ancient and abandoned equipment. Fortunately it was recognised as the historic Marconi House transmitter notwithstanding its dismantled state. However it was complete; and John

Gilman, the Brookmans Park engineer who discovered it, re-assembled the transmitter back in the main building having carefully dried out the parts. One night, after closedown, the old transmitter worked into the Brookmans Park aerial. It operated successfully, the staff being impressed by the brilliance of the large valves (John Gilman writing in *Ariel (BBC House Magazine)*, 12 September 1981). For a few months in 1992 the veteran transmitter was on display in the entrance hall of Broadcasting House in connection with the 70th Anniversary celebrations.

Until mid-1925, the BBC stations could only serve predominantly urban populations, the low-power transmitters being located in the major cities. In an attempt to remedy this imbalance, the BBC requested permission from the Postmaster-General to build a powerful 25kW long-wave station at Daventry in Northamptonshire. ▶ The site was a 650ft hill of great historic significance known as Borough Hill. The aerial was held aloft by two triangulated steel masts 500ft tall and set 800ft apart. The station's programmes were received by land-line from Savoy Hill and re-radiated. The programmes were to all intents identical to those of 2LO. 5XX Daventry was the most powerful broadcasting station in the world and the first to use long-wave

* Transmitter engineers relished the rooftop cafe and garden, Selfridges proving very hospitable in looking after them.

▶ In November 1926 the Postmaster-General granted permission for the Station to be increased in power from 25kW to 30kW.

transmission. Its signals were able to reach out across much of rural England bringing the wonderful miracle of wireless to the remote and backward-looking rural communities. Its opening on 27 July 1925 greatly impressed all those present. Even hardened reporters waxed lyrical. 'Here outside in the night air all was quiet. Silence - and yet one felt the mystery of those invisible waves; the miracle of the hidden voices sweeping out through the night ... "Daventry Calling... Daventry Calling"". (Leslie Baily: Briggs - I, p. 224).

(reproduced by permission of the Marconi Company, Ltd.)

2LO transmitter, Selfridges, 1925

THE COMPANY GIVES WAY TO THE CORPORATION AND THE SAVOY HILL COUNTDOWN BEGINS

I. THE NEW CORPORATION

SH-SUMMARY: Entry - 23: February 1927. Small ground floor room opposite the lift at the West Entrance, formerly an IEE telephoning room, given to BBC as a waiting room, on condition that the BBC constructed a telephone box in the IEE Building in exchange.

The administrative entrance to the BBC in Company days was very much a side entrance: narrow steps between iron railings bridged a dismal Basement passage. As the Company gained new Corporation status at the end of 1926, a more fitting introduction was felt to be essential. A tall stone-clad entrance took

the place of the old one and new wider steps with flanking low stone walls carried the architectural effect forward to the pavement. These walls bore the 'BBC' monogram set in an incised circle. Inside, the acquisition of the IEE telephone room provided not so much a 'waiting room' as a lobby with perhaps a small enquiry point for visitors.

This rather minor physical change marked the coming of the Corporation and was paralleled by equally low-key changes in organisation and staffing. The Controller now took over responsibility for International Relations with a special Section reporting to him. But more significant was the BBC's release from the restrictions imposed at the request of the press in 1922. Eye-witness accounts and running commentaries could now be broadcast and this greatly extended the work of the Talks Department and OB

Corinthians v Newcastle United at Crystal Palace; outside broadcast, January, 1927

Oxford & Cambridge Boat Race, March, 1927; transmitter installed on *The Magician*
(*reproduced by permission of the BBC*)

engineers. The England v Wales rugger match at Twickenham was broadcast on 15 January 1927 marking a new era in wireless. The Open Golf Championship, the Cup Final at Wembley, the Boat Race, the Derby, Trooping the Colour and Wimbledon followed in quick succession (West, p.23). A new member of staff - Hilda Matheson - became Director of Talks and News, Stobart's responsibility now being limited to Education. But this was itself expanding to include adult education, the latter headed by another newcomer, R. S. Lambert.

But the major re-organisation had already occurred earlier in 1926. There were five main 'Branches' or 'Divisions' each under an 'Assistant Controller' - Programmes, Information, Engineering, Secretariat and Finance. Within each were a number of 'Departments' headed by 'Directors' and these in turn often comprised two or more 'Sections'. The 1926 organisation, still relevant to the early Corporation years, is set out in Appendix C. The 'Programmes' and 'Information' Branches were housed in Savoy Hill Mansions and the layout of their accommodation has been described in Chapter IV. We can now consider how the Secretariat and Finance Branches were housed in the IEE building. Once again the guide is the *BBC Staff Directory* issued in December 1926.

Within the IEE Building, the key functional change since January 1924 was the exodus of the programme and publicity staff from the North Wing in June to September 1925. They were accompanied by the London Station staff and the Music Department. This left the IEE Building largely available for Management, Secretariat and Finance.

The prestigious South Wing now became the preserve of the Heads of the Secretariat and Finance Divisions and their Deputies. Here they had easy access to the Board Room and the Management suite. The Registrar and Cashier Sections had to transfer to the North Wing to make way for these new dignitaries and the post of Company Secretary was abolished at the same time.

Apart from the studios, the space at first and third floor levels was occupied by the Engineering Division, though with Rooms 5/6 serving as a Band Room for Studio - I. The North Wing provided accommodation for a new Technical Correspondence Department under R. Wynn who had joined the BBC in early 1926 along with Noël Ashbridge, who became Deputy to P. P. Eckersley. All three had been 'Writtle' pioneers operating the pre-BBC experimental Marconi service in 1922 from an ex-Army hut at Writtle, near Chelmsford, Essex, where the Marconi Works was situated.

The enlargement and re-organisation of the third floor Control Room in November 1925 has already been described (Chapter IV, Section 6). It did not affect office space. At Basement level the Central Stores (Campbell) were transferred in 1926 to the eastern end of the Mansions basement, being replaced by a Works Store (Patmore) for the more prosaic items of equipment. The North Room of the IEE basement was still occupied by the Engineering Workshop (Midson).

The transition from Company to Corporation thus saw few major accommodation changes and even fewer organisational ones except at top management level. With the swing from private to public status some staff feared for their jobs, as indeed they might today in similar, or more probably, reverse circumstances. But they need not have done so for none were lost. For the BBC it was quite simply a time to celebrate four years of outstandingly successful growth and its coming of age as a 'public corporation' - something quite new to Britain in 1926. *

On the eve of this great event - Friday evening, 31 December 1926 - employees were all invited to attend a dance given by the old BBC in the magnificent Hotel Cecil hard by Savoy

* Reith was subsequently a great advocate of the 'public Corporation ' model, applying it to Imperial Airways in 1940 (British Overseas Airways Corporation), to New Towns in 1946 and later to Commonwealth Development. Other early examples were the Central Electricity Board responsible for the 'grid', and the London Passenger Transport Board.

Hill. One of the senior staff recalled it as 'all very gay and merry. To everybody's astonishment there was not only a bar, but a free bar, with spirits flowing like water'. On Monday morning 'everybody was telling stories of the party and how tight everybody else had been. Everybody seemed to have taken somebody else home and, if you compared the stories, some of them must have been taking each other home. The British Broadcasting Company may have come in like a lamb but it went out with a bang' (Gorham, p. 26).

(reproduced by permission of the BBC)

2. DISPERSAL FROM SAVOY HILL AND FINAL FAREWELL

SH-SUMMARY: Entries - 21, 25 to 27 and 29 to 43: July 1927/May 1932. Civil Engineer instructed by Control Board to look round for a site for a future Broadcasting House, the accommodation question being extremely acute (July 1927).

DISPERSAL:

Space in No. 10 Savoy Street taken (in three stages starting September 1926).

28/29 Southampton Street rented (September 1927)

Space in Cecil Chambers, Strand, taken (in eight stages starting September 1928).

Space in 34/35 Southampton Street taken (March 1929)

Space in 42 Maiden Lane, Covent Garden, taken (June 1930)

Occupied premises at Big Tree Wharf beside the old Waterloo Bridge (south end). Transformed into No. 10 Studio, the largest then possessed by the BBC (October 1930).

MOVE TO BROADCASTING HOUSE:

Move to Broadcasting House began. All Cecil Chambers and Southampton Street staffs were transferred and some Head Office staff (September 1931).

The big move took place spread over four weekends - 2/3 April, 16/17 April, 23/24 April, 30 April/1 May. All staff left Savoy Hill except a few engineers to handle the farewell programme (April 1932).

'End of Savoy Hill' programme. After the programme was finished, D.G. (the Director-General, Sir John Reith) locked the door of the main (West) entrance for the last time after everyone had left (14 May 1932).

With the transition from company to Corporation, Savoy Hill had attained its apogee with all its Head Office staff still within the one building group along with the staff of 2LO the London Station, save only the two or three engineers manning the transmitter on the roof of Selfridges. The Savoy Hill staff now approached 400 and dealt with every aspect of broadcasting. Here 'the working of twenty-one stations was co-ordinated; here questions of administration, policy

and finance were settled. Broad questions of programme policy, including music, education and drama, were discussed. Finance, stores and buying were centralised. Technical research and development was carried out. Technical correspondence was dealt with, including oscillation reports, etc. BBC publications, such as the *Radio Times*, *World Radio*, opera libretti, National and other BBC concert programmes - all had a home in this building. An Information Department spent busy days here. Workshops in various parts of the building dealt with calls for specialised equipment or its alteration, repair and assembly. The Outside Broadcast engineers had their own room full of equipment ready to be rushed off to any part of the country in their own van'. (H. L. Chilman, *Wireless World*, 30 March 1927). Added to all this was the host of artistes and potential broadcasters pouring daily into the nine studios to take part in auditions, rehearsals and the programmes that daily fed the 2LO and 5XX transmitters, the more important of which were relayed by land-line to other stations.

This variety of activities and humanity helped to give a sense of improvised spontaneity, and therefore of informality, to Savoy Hill which left a deep impression on those who were there. In its lifts and on its staircases 'the poet rubs shoulders with the soubrette, the Archdeacon with the football specialist, the actor with the engineer. Happily the air on Savoy Hill is not too rarefied: close at hand are two vast hotels full of bustling Americans (Savoy Hotel/Hotel Cecil); before it flows the water of the Thames and the trams on the Embankment. The roar of Strand traffic, with motor cars hooting and grinding of brakes, is never quite silent in its offices'. (*BBC Handbook*, 1929, p. 252).

All this noise and bustle served to remind the artistes and the busy staff of the great mass of humanity - listening humanity - which extended out in all directions from the secure boundaries of their hallowed precinct.

The changeover from Company to Corporation did nothing to stem the headlong growth of the BBC but it did mark the limit in the capacity of Savoy Hill to cope with this growth. Within a few months, the BBC's Head of Premises - Marmaduke Tudsbery - was instructed to think about a new headquarters and to find a suitable site. His task, and the design and construction of the new purpose-built Broadcasting House, would take five years .

In the meantime, with staff growing at a hundred annually, it became urgently necessary to take any accommodation that might become available in the vicinity - in Savoy Street (across the road from the IEE); in Southampton Street/Maiden Lane just across the Strand; and in nearby Cecil Chambers. But there was also a more substantial dispersal with the move of the Research and Development Departments (Engineering Division) to Clapham. Never again would the BBC's specialist, management and production activities be housed in one building group. With dispersal something of the old collegiate atmosphere began to dissolve. In the end some 250 staff were scattered

about Savoy Hill's environs. They were, in fact, the first to enter Broadcasting House taking up their new offices in September 1931.

Finally the great move from Savoy Hill itself took place. It was spread over four weekends in April 1932. For many staff it must have seemed a great wrench, especially for those who had joined the BBC in Company days and had occupied the same room for the intervening period of five or more years. This particularly applied to senior staff like the Controller, Admiral Carpendale, and Lochhead, the Chief Accountant, both still in their original IEE Building rooms at the end of Savoy Hill days. Similarly, Gladstone Murray, Head of Information, and R. H. Eckersley, Head of Programmes, who found themselves bidding farewell to their offices in the Mansions where, since 1925, they had enjoyed looking on to the historic seclusion of the Savoy Chapel and Churchyard where the starlings warned them the end of the day had come. Reith himself owned to feeling 'affection for the old place', and found moral support from having eighteen veteran survivors by him when he first spoke to the staff in the new Broadcasting House. These veterans had accompanied him into Savoy Hill on the very first day - 19 March 1923 (Briggs - II, p. 459). By contrast, those who had inhabited the *Radio Times* offices on the east side of the Mansions may have been less wedded to their accommodation; they had endured two years of dust and the staccato noise of pneumatic drills as the buildings over the tram tunnel were pulled down and the gleaming bulk of Brettenham House rose across the road.

More evocative than the desertion of rooms, was the removal and scrapping of equipment that had done such good service in the Control Room, Studios and the curious 'Studio - 2E' - the Effects Room in the Basement. This final clearance had of course to await the 'Farewell' broadcast and formal evacuation booked for the 14 May.

The BBC were perhaps a little self-conscious about their move. But immediately after the event they relaxed their guard. Arthur Watts illustrated the move for the *Radio Times* (special Broadcasting House number, 18 May 1932). He pictured it as a 'cavalcade from Savoy Hill to Broadcasting House' headed by the BBC Military Band; immediately behind came the 'Queen of the Typists' leading the office cats who in turn were jumping up on to the float transporting sound-effects experts in the throes of imitating nightingales. Announcers announcing preceded a veiled yet top-hatted figure on horseback (A. J. Alan, the mystery broadcaster). His horse drew a triumphal car on which the 'Spirit of Broadcasting' addressed an attentive Britannia. They were followed by a fiercely serious group of 'eminent broadcasters' headed by a rather daunting woman. A final allegorical carriage bore the slogan 'Home, Sweet Home' and exhibited a typical family quietly listening-in, the carriage being pulled by BBC office boys disguised as cupids. The procession wound up with chained 'interferers' - those who had ignored pleas not to 'oscillate' - in the

charge of the winged 'Spirit of Detection' holding a flaming torch.

The last day was 14 May 1932. At 9.20 p.m. listeners heard a voice amid a fanfare of trumpets announce 'The End of Savoy Hill, an historical pageant in sound covering 1922 to 1932 - ten years of broadcasting in one hundred and sixty one and a half minutes'. The second part of this 'farewell' programme was made up with a tour of the Savoy Hill studios, flashbacks illustrating the kind of programmes normally broadcast from each. Some of these had been previously recorded by the Blattnerphone (Stille) process on steel tape. The programme ended with Big Ben striking Midnight. Except, that is, for a few last sounds.

Hibberd describes how a group of engineers, having closed down the Savoy Hill Control Room for the last time, descended the steps to the main entrance 'followed by myself [in] conversation with Oliver, the night-watchman' (Hibberd, p. 73). Listeners could hear their footsteps and they heard Oliver remove the iron shutter and open the small door in it to let them out into the street. "Well, Oliver, I suppose this is the last time you'll be pulling down that old shutter for me". "Yes, Sir," he replied; "this is the end of Savoy Hill ... mind your head, sir".

With these words, Savoy Hill became silent and still and virtually uninhabited, except for the great flocks of twittering starlings arriving at sundown to roost in the trees of the churchyard. But, within two years, as though conscious of the dark, cold emptiness of the buildings, they too deserted the precinct.

Reith locks up after the last programme *(reproduced by permission of the BBC)*

3. TO BROADCASTING HOUSE AND STERN REALITY

Few would recognise Broadcasting House as the offspring of Savoy Hill. There could hardly be a greater contrast in either appearance or character. To an extent these contrasts were the fruit of circumstances. Broadcasting House was purpose-designed. Savoy Hill had been conceived as a Medical Examination Hall with an apartment block to the rear. But in each case the character of the BBC organisation was at one with the physical environment that surrounded and housed it. It is difficult to know which influenced the other the more.

For the BBC, the Savoy Hill era was marked by growth from humble and uncertain beginnings. The organisation stumbled with faltering steps almost from year to year in the early 'twenties and was subjected to probing Government reviews in 1923 and again in 1925. Only in 1927 did it receive full recognition as a new type of national institution worthy to become established by Royal Charter. With the decision to build its own house, the BBC not unnaturally chose to proclaim its new dignified and permanent status. The preferred location amid the stately formality of Portland Place reflected the new ethos. Not for the BBC the commercialism of the City nor the razzmatazz of Soho, Covent Garden or Fleet Street. The site selected - Langham Place at the end of Portland Place - was both respectable and prominent: it closed the vista at the end

of London's finest shopping street, Regent Street. On its doorstep, a church; on its flank a concert hall - a cultural *cachet* particularly appropriate at a time when the BBC Symphony Orchestra was in the process of formation. For the BBC had taken to itself a high ideal: it saw itself as The Sower 'broadcasting' the good seed and looking forward to the harvest. A sculpture depicting 'The Sower' was given pride of place in the new entrance hall and an inscription carved in stone over the statue echoed the theme.

Looking forward seemed to be the keynote. It was reflected in the design of the building and especially in that of its interior. The decor of the studios, Green Rooms and principal offices was, by and large, light years away from Savoy Hill. Elaborate control panels bristling with knobs; windows peering down into studios from Silence Rooms; the cold, bizarre apparatus in the Effects Studio: all looked like sets for a futuristic film. Everything was planned down to the last detail to create an elaborate but beautiful machine.

As planning came in, improvisation went out. The jostling of staff and artistes in the congested corridors of Savoy Hill would not be replicated in Broadcasting House. No more rubbing shoulders with A. J. Alan, the story-teller, Leonard Henry, Wynne Ajello, Claude Hulbert and Enid Trevor, Scott and Whaley, Flotsam and Jetsam, Ronald Gourley and Jack Payne of the BBC Dance Orchestra (Gorham, p.33). In the new quarters at Langham Place, all such artistes were securely isolated in a tower of studios approached from its own lifts and stairs.

Gone too were the muddled days when 'everyone was ready to do everyone else's job' (R. H. Eckersley, p.58). Each member of staff now had his or her place in the complex broadcasting machine and was required to keep pace with it.

It may be that Reith was himself a victim of the new building and the imperatives it imposed; but was he perhaps a willing victim, half in love with the new regime and the kudos it afforded? Addressing the assembled staff in the new building for the first time he declared his 'affection for the old place' (Savoy Hill). But he went on resolutely ... 'I do not regret the past, because regretting [the loss of] the past is a great mistake. I look forward; nothing but forward'. (Briggs - II, p. 465). The assembled staff got the message. With a heavy heart old hands passed it on to the young ones for, from now, all must toe the line:

When the BBC was young, lad,
And all its branches green,
When studios were draped, lad,
'Effects' better heard than seen
'Twas Heigh' for homely cheer, lad,
Gas fires and cosy tea
And bright ideas and hopes, lad,
For the future yet to be.

In the BBC today, lad,
Just through its first decade,
With many a member missing
From the ranks of the 'Old Brigade'
'Tis stand not upon your going,
But strive to keep the pace,
For the dream is a stern reality,
Broadcasting House in Langham Place.

M. E. E.
21 March 1933

(From *The Heterodyne, the BBC Staff Magazine*, May 1933)

THE LEGACY

SAVOY HILL TODAY

Like the BBC staff of the 'twenties we can approach Savoy Hill from two main directions. One way lies through the Embankment Gardens from the direction of Embankment Station. 'The shaven lawns, gay bulbs and the little corner where the fountain is an oasis of spangled shade' provide as peaceful an approach for us today as for Peter Eckersley writing in 1924 (*Radio Times*, 11 January issue). We come out into Savoy Place and turn left up Savoy Hill to the Institution's West Entrance at No. 2. Here the great mass of the flank of the Savoy Hotel overshadows the little street giving it an air of dreary seclusion.

Or we can approach Savoy Hill from the Strand, still a roaring thoroughfare focused on St Mary-le-Strand's baroque steeple. Just short of the church a little side street dips down past the church-yard of the Savoy Chapel and, immediately behind its trees, Savoy Hill Mansions rises like a sentinel in late-Victorian attire presenting its two entrances to the street. The atmosphere of the precinct is very pronounced and the appearance of the buildings is much as it was in BBC days.

Today there are few survivors of the BBC's Savoy Hill era to remind us that this little precinct was once a nerve-centre for the nation with ambitions, even in the early 'Company' years, to serve the Empire by circling the globe. For a brief spell in the long history of the twentieth century, the windows of Savoy Hill lit up each evening like a hundred glowing valves. Through the ether, companionship and pleasure were conveyed to millions of people, people whose memories of 2LO persisted long after the actual passing. Indeeed, much of what evolved seventy years ago at Savoy Hill remains with us today.

Savoy Hill deserves to be remembered and celebrated; for it was from Savoy Hill that the 'Spirit of Broadcasting' first addressed an attentive Britannia.

Appendix A

SOURCES USED

The BBC Written Archives Centre appear to have no plans of the Savoy Hill Buildings occupied during 'Company' years (1923 to 1926). The Archives of the Institution of Electrical Engineers however include the following drawings which proved helpful:

Plans and Sections of the IEE building as originally constructed in 1886/89, along with plans showing the reconstruction of the lecture hall and entrance which were prepared by Percy Adams, architects for the IEE in 1909 when the Institution purchased the building and took up occupation.

Pre-BBC plans of the surviving portion of Savoy Hill Mansions, but showing the proposed layout for the re-building of the western portion ('North West Building'). These plans were prepared by Mewes and Davis, architects, in October 1924 for the BBC and show initial proposals for the allocation of space in the North West Building and arrangements for forming a connecting passage to the IEE Building.

Plan prepared by the BBC in 1926 for the layout of the Basement of the Mansions.

It will be evident that few of these plans related directly to the BBC's occupation or to the way this changed over the period of the 'Company' years. The BBC's Written Archives Centre was, however, able to provide a document headed *Savoy Hill: Summary* which describes the expansion in occupancy in a series of brief dated entries of which no less than twenty relate to the Company years.

Whilst the *SH-Summary* has references to buildings and the dates of opening, there is little indication of how the space was occupied or by whom. However this gap was filled, at least for 1923, by two little sketch plans dated July and November respectfully, which the W. A. C. provided. These showed existing and proposed allocation of rooms to named officers or functions. These sketch layouts became meaningful only when they were compared with the IEE drawings.

Another W. A. C. document dates from the end of the Company period and comprises a list of senior staff and their secretaries - 132 named staff. The purpose of the list is to give the room and telephone numbers. The Staff List includes the following functional entries:

GENERAL/ADMIN

Messengers (Post Room)
Duplicating (Room - 38)
Enquiries (North/West/East Entrances)
Filing (G.O./Room - 37)
General Office
Post Room (G.O.)
Telephone S-Board (Room - 21)

ENGINEERING

Amplifier Room (= Control Room) (Room - 23)
Central Stores (Basement)
Lines Section (Room - 74)
Research (Room - 31)
Workshop (Basement)

The problem was how to relate the room numbers to the plans. The way this problem was overcome is set out in Chapter IV, (Section 4). The staff list in augmented form is set out in Appendix D below.

Old photographs provided additional evidence as to which rooms served particular functions. The BBC collection was particularly helpful but, of the BBC photographs taken during the Savoy Hill decade, less than one in ten relate to the Company years. However, apart from the more obvious views of studios the collection includes excellent coverage of Control Room and other equipment. Pictures of offices are virtually non-existent.

For other sources which have been referred to in compiling this account see Appendix B.

Appendix B

BIBLIOGRAPHY

Use has been made of the following books and periodicals all of which are contemporary with the period of the BBC's occupation of Savoy Hill:

Cecil LEWIS: Broadcasting from within (Newnes, 1924)
Arthur BURROWS: The Story of Broadcasting (Cassell, 1924)
J. C. W. REITH: Broadcast over Britain (Hodder & Stoughton, 1924)
Art and Technique of Broadcasting (Marconi Wireless Telegraph Company, 1924)
Broadcast Listeners' Year Book 1924 (Radio Press, 1924)
BBC Handbooks and Year Books, 1928- (BBC)
Wireless Annual for Amateurs and Experimenters, 1924 (Wireless Press).
Marconi-Sykes Magnetophone with details of the Amplifiers: article by Capt. H. J. Round (*Wireless World*, 26 November 1924)
The Battery Room at 2LO: Article by A. C. Shaw (*Wireless World*, 24 March 1926)
A Tour round Savoy Hill: a series of seven articles by A. G. D. West; A. C. Shaw; A. S. Attkins and H. L. Chilman (*Wireless World*, 9 February/30 March 1927)
Savoy Hill with the Lid Off: a series of five articles (*Radio Times*, 6 April, 20 April, 4 May, 25 May, 15 June 1928).

Other early sources include:

Garry ALLIGHAN: Sir John Reith (Stanley Paul, 1938)
W. GOATMAN: By-ways of the BBC (P. S. King & Son, 1938)
Lance SIEVEKING: The Stuff of Radio (Cassell, 1934)
A. C. SHAW: Early Days of Broadcasting (*World Radio*, 15 November 1935)

A number of post-war and more recent general histories of the BBC have provided useful information on the 'Company' period, in particular:

Twenty-Five Years of British Broadcasting (BBC, 1947)
Asa BRIGGS: History of Broadcasting in the United Kingdom. Volume I: The Birth of Broadcasting (covers the Company Years). Volume II: The Golden Age of Wireless (covers 1927 to 1939) (Oxford University Press, 1961 and 1965)
K. GEDDES: Broadcasting in Britain (HMSO, 1972)

E. PAWLEY: BBC Engineering, 1922 to 1972 (BBC, 1972)
Val GIELGUD: British Radio Drama, 1922 to 1956 (Harrap, 1957)
P. E. WEST: BBC Engineering: the First Five Years (*BBC Engineering* No. 92) (BBC, 1972)
Susan BRIGGS: Those Radio Times (Weidenfeld & Nicolson, 1981)
R. APPLEYARD: History of the Institution of Electrical Engineers (IEE, 1939)
N. KENYON: BBC Symphony Orchestra, 1930 - 1980 (BBC, 1981)

Some of the senior staff of Savoy Hill days subsequently wrote books outlining their careers in broadcasting. These often have illuminating and, sometimes amusing, references to Savoy Hill and help to convey what it was like to work there:

Jack PAYNE: This is Jack Payne (Sampson Low, Marston, 1932)
Richard S. LAMBERT: Ariel and all his Quality: an impression of the BBC from within (Victor Gollancz, 1940)
R. ECKERSLEY: BBC and All That (Sampson Low, Marston, 1946)
Maurice GORHAM: Sound and Fury (Percival Marshall, 1948)
Stuart HIBBERD: This - is London (Macdonald & Evans, 1950)
Freddie GRISEWOOD: The World Goes By (Martin Secker & Warburg, 1953)
Eric MASCHWITZ: No Chip on my Shoulder (Herbert Jenkins, 1957)
John SNAGGE *and* Michael BARSLEY: Those Vintage Years of Radio (Pitman, 1972)

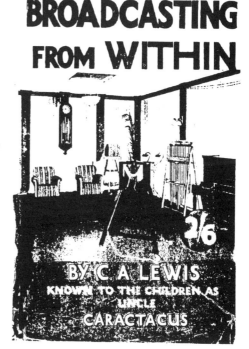

First Studio, 1923 Ceiling and hangings were in gold, carpet in blue, and armchairs gold and blue stripes
(*reproduced by permission of George Newnes*)

Appendix C

BBC HEAD OFFICE ORGANISATION: DECEMBER 1926

Below are listed the Departments and Sections comprising the five Divisions of the BBC organisation as it existed at the end of Company days. Much of this organisation remained in place after the Corporation took over on 1st January 1927 and, indeed, until the re-organisation of 1933. The main change in January 1927 in terms of staffing was the creation of separate Departments for Talks and Education the duties being distributed as follows:

TALKS

News/SOS's
Talks
Eye Witness Accounts
Running Commentaries

EDUCATION

Children's Hour
Executive
Booking
Appeals/Church Services
Schools/Literature
Schools Engineers
Adult Education

The Heads of Divisions ranked as 'Assistant Controllers' though some retained their earlier titles as Director of Programmes, Chief Engineer and Chief Accountant. The term 'Director' tended to be applied to heads of Departments and served to identify these as Departments rather than Sections.

The London Head Office - Savoy Hill - included about half the total staff of the BBC in December 1926, that is 375/400 out of a total 773.

The following schedule is based on the Organisation Chart in *The Birth of Broadcasting* by Asa Briggs (OUP, 1961). It is reproduced by permission of Oxford University Press:

MANAGING DIRECTOR (DIRECTOR GENERAL from 1 January 1927)

CONTROLLER

Foreign Relations (from 1 January 1927)

INFORMATION DIVISION (Gladstone Murray)

Deputy
EXECUTIVE
DISTRICT LIAISON
LECTURES/PHOTOGRAPHS/VISITORS
INTELLIGENCE (inc. Records/Library/Press)
PRESS
PUBLICATIONS (inc. Advertising)
RADIO TIMES
WORLD RADIO

SECRETARIAT OR ADMINISTRATION DIVISION (V.H. Goldsmith)

Deputy
REGISTRAR/PRINTING/STATIONARY
INTERNAL ADMINISTRATION/GENERAL OFFICE/FILING
PERSONNEL/PAYMENT

FINANCE DIVISION (T. Lochhead)

Deputy
CASH
STANDING CHARGES
PURCHASE (inc. Buying/Requisitions and Invoices)
RECORDS
LIAISON BETWEEN H.O. AND PROVINCIAL STATIONS

PROGRAMMES DIVISION (R. Eckersley)

Deputy
EDUCATION/TALKS (inc. Talks and Local News/Children's Hour/Executive and 'Follow up'/ Booking Appeals and Church Services/Schools and Literature/Schools Engineers)

MUSIC (inc. Balance and Control/Orchestra/Executive/Chorus/Music Library and Hiring)

EXECUTIVE (inc. Finance/Copyright/Central Booking/Programme Correspondence/SB and *Radio Times*)

PRODUCTIONS (inc. Variety and Revue/Dramatic Rehearsals and Productions/Effects, Written Material and Play Records/Play Reading and Adapting)

LONDON STATION (inc. O.B./Programmes/Studios/Announcers)

ENGINEERING DIVISION (P. P. Eckersley)

Deputy
DEVELOPMENT
LINES
RESEARCH
TECHNICAL CORRESPONDENCE/INFORMATION
EQUIPMENT
PREMISES AND FIXTURES
MAINTENANCE (North and South)
O.B.

No. 8 Studio, Savoy Hill (reproduced by permission of the BBC)

Appendix D

STAFF LIST/ROOM ALLOCATION: DECEMBER 1926

Reference has been made in Appendix A to the document in the BBC W. A. C. listing staff, their room numbers and internal telephone numbers. This list is dated December 1926. The list includes about a hundred senior staff and their secretaries. We know that Savoy Hill staff numbered 335 in early May and this number would have grown to 375 or more by the end of December. The Staff List therefore covers only a third of the total staff.

    Although issued as an alphabetical list, the names are rearranged below by order of room number. In addition, the posts held have been added where these are known from other sources. The relevant plan number is shown.

ROOM NO.	OFFICER (SECRETARY)	POST HELD

IEE BUILDING

West Wing: First Floor: South (ENGINEERING) (PLAN 8b)

1	P. P. Eckersley	A. C. Engineering
2	(Fortune)	
3	H. Bishop	Dir. Maintenance
	(Cockerton)	
4	N. Ashbridge	Dep. Engineering Div'n
	(Williams)	

West Wing: Second Floor: South (MANAGEMENT) (PLAN 8c)

7	J. C. W. Reith	Man. Director
8	Miss I. Shields	Priv. Sec'y to M.D.
	Miss E. M. Nash	Priv. Sec'y to Cont'r
9	C. D. Carpendale	Controller

South Wing: Second Floor (SECRETARIAT/FINANCE) (PLAN 8c)

13	V. H. Goldsmith	A. C. Secretariat
	(Freeman)	
14	R. Wade	Dep. Secretariat Div'n
15	W. H. Harley	Dep. Finance Div'n
	(Chilton)	
15A	T. Lochhead	A. C. Finance
	(Lock)	

North Wing: Second Floor (SECRETARIAT/FINANCE) (PLAN 8c)

16	G. H. Dunbar	Publications Accounts
	R. G. Fudge	
17	Miss I. F. Mallinson	Assistant Cashier
	J. Dormer	Chief Cashier
18	R. M. Page	Stationery
	F. E. Walker	Registrar
19	G. Strode	Publications Accounts (?)
20	H. W. Boyce	

North Wing: Third Floor (ENGINEERING) (PLAN 8d)

24	F. M. Dimmock	Dir. Equipment
	J. F. Baugh	Buying
25	G. Alderson	
	C. R. Wade	Programme Correspondence
26	T. G. Carter	Technical Inform'n/Corresp.
27	R. Wynn	Dir. Tech. Inform'n/Corresp.
	(Haynes)	
27A	H. A. Hankey	Technical Inform'n/Corresp.

Other Named Staff:

G. O.	Miss C. Banks	General Office/Filing (PLAN 8c)
	(Hills)	
	(Fitzgerald)	Post Room

SAVOY HILL MANSIONS

Fifth Floor (ENGINEERING) (PLAN 10c)

29A	H. L. Kirke	Dir. Eng. Development
	L. W. Hayes	Eng. Development
31	-	Eng. Research

Fourth Floor (INFORMATION) (PLAN 10b)

33	Miss F. Milnes	Library (?)
34	Gladstone Murray	A.C. Information
	(Dods)	
35	T. J. Hawtayne	Dep. Information Div'n
	(Lyons)	

36	B. B. Chapman	Press
37	(Gorry)	Filing
38	(Lucy)	Duplicating
39	G. V. Rice	Publications
	(Potigar)	
40	C. F. Atkinson	International
41	M. Gorham	*Radio Times*
42	W. G. Fuller	Editor *Radio Times*
	(King)	
43	Miss J. Bryant	*Radio Times*
	P. W. Darnell	*Radio Times* News
	C. Tristram	*Radio Times* Programmes
	G. H. Hodder	*Radio Times* Programmes
	N. D. Slatter	*Radio Times* Programmes
44	Mrs E. Fitzgerald	*World Radio*
	Lynch Odhams	Editor *World Radio*
45	Mrs K. Lines	Photographic Library
45A	J. H. Whitehouse	
46	R. Gambier-Parry	Dir. Publications
	(Gomm)	

Third Floor (PROGRAMMES/LONDON STATION) (PLAN 10a)

47A	R. H. Eckersley	A. C. Programmes
47	(Jockel)	
48	C. G. Graves	Dep. Programmes Div'n
	R. J. Howgill	Copyright
49	P. E. Cruttwell	Dir. Programmes Executive
	(Lowden)	
51	Miss M. Somerville	Schools
	(Ussher)	
51A	J. C. Stobart	Dir. Education/Talks
	(Playle)	
52	L. Sieveking	Topical Talks
	F. Strutt	Local News
	J. S. Dodgson	
	(Sprott)	
53	B. E. Nicolls	Dir. London Station
	(Tone)	
54	R. E. Wellington	London. Station Programmes
	(Kelly)	
55	E. Maschwitz	Outside Broadcasts

55A	G. A. Cock (Clark)	Dir. Outside Broadcasts
56	D. Millar Craig	Music Editor *Radio Times*
	L. Stanton Jefferies	Music: Balance/Control
57	K.A. Wright (D. Wood)	Prog. Exec: Music
57A	P. Pitt	Dir. Music
58	S. Hibberd	London Station Chief Announcer
	V. Hely Hutchinson (Godwin)	London Station Orchestra
59	C. E. Hodges	Dir. Children's Hour
	Miss E. Elliott	Children's Hour
60	T. C. Farrar	London Station Announcer
	J. T. Sutthery	Simultaneous Broadcasting
62	A. C. Shaw	Dir. Control Room
	A. G. Dryland	Control Room

Second Floor (PLAN 13c)

66	A. G. D. West (Griffiths)	Dir. Eng. Research
67	(Taylor)	
67A	R. Palmer	Programmes Booking
68	M. J. Corridan	
	P. Tillett	
69	P. A. Florence (Garnett)	Maintenance South (?) Eng. Admin (?)
69A	A. Wynn	Music Contracts (?)
	J. F. Barham (Minns)	
70	M. Tudsbery	Dir. Premises/Fixed Equipmt.
71	F. Holland	Premises/Fixed Equipmt.
74	A. S. Attkins	Dir. S.B. Lines

First Floor (PLAN 13b)

| 84 | Mrs H. S. Waterman | Music Library |
| 85 | F. Hook | Dir. Music Library/Hiring |

Ground Floor (PROGRAMMES/LONDON STATION) (PLAN 13a)

88	L. Spurling	Announcers
90	R. E. Jeffrey (Glasby)	Dir. Productions
91	J. E. Sharman	Variety/Revue
	A. Whitman	Dramatic Effects
	K. V. Wright	Play Reading
92	B. Fryer	Variety/Revue
	J. H. Macdonell	Surprise Items
	H. Rose	Producer of Plays
94	Thompson	O.B. Engineer
95A	R. Judson	Publications Advertising
96	S. Firman	Dance Orchestra
	S. Kneale Kelly	London Station Orchestra
	Stanford Robinson	London Station Chorus
	F. Dickie	Secretary London Station Orchestra
	J. Ansell	Conductor London Station Orchestra
98	H. L. Chilman	House Supt./Studio Booking

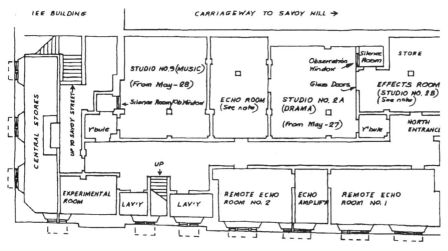

IEE BUILDING   CARRIAGEWAY TO SAVOY HILL →

CENTRAL STORES

UP TO SAVOY STREET →

STUDIO NO.9 (MUSIC) (From May-28)

Silence Room/Ob.Window

ECHO ROOM (See note)

Observation Window

Glass Doors

Silence Room

STORE

EFFECTS ROOM (STUDIO NO. 2B) (See note)

STUDIO NO. 2A (DRAMA) (From May-27)

Y'bule

NORTH ENTRANCE

Y'bule

EXPERIMENTAL ROOM

UP

LAV'Y   LAV'Y

REMOTE ECHO ROOM NO. 2

ECHO AMPLIF'R

REMOTE ECHO ROOM NO. 1

NOTE

Studio No. 2B was later re-numbered 2E (for 'Effects'). The Echo Room was numbered 2F (for 'Gramophone') as it was equipped with a gramophone for producing recorded effects and incidental music for plays.

SAVOY HILL MANSIONS Basement

(May - 27/May -28)

105

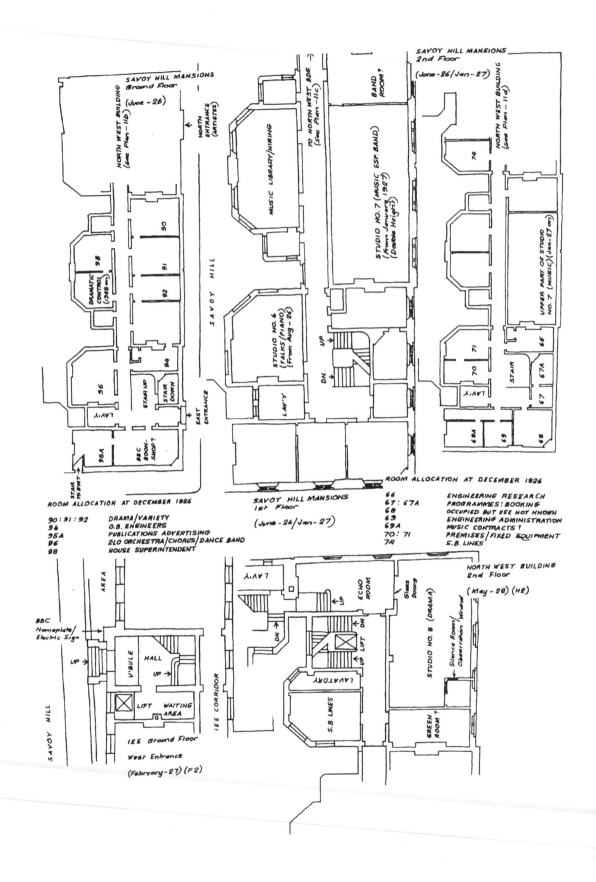

SAVOY HILL MANSIONS
Ground Floor
(June - 26)

NORTH WEST BUILDING
(See Plan - 11b)

SAVOY HILL MANSIONS
2nd Floor
(June-26/Jan-27)

NORTH WEST BUILDING
(See Plan - 11d)

NORTH
ENTRANCE
(ARTISTES)

98

DRAMATIC
CONTROL
(358 sq.)

90

91

92

96

94

STAIR UP

STAIR
DOWN

LAV'Y

95A

BBC
BOOK-
SHOP?

EAST
ENTRANCE

STAIR
TO BWY

SAVOY HILL

ROOM ALLOCATION AT DECEMBER 1926

90:91:92   DRAMA/VARIETY
94   O.B. ENGINEERS
95A   PUBLICATIONS ADVERTISING
96   2LO ORCHESTRA/CHORUS/DANCE BAND
98   HOUSE SUPERINTENDENT

MUSIC LIBRARY/HIRING

TO NORTH WEST BLDG.
(See Plan - 11c)

BAND
ROOM?

STUDIO NO. 7 (MUSIC ESP BAND)
(From January 1927)
(Double Height)

STUDIO NO. 6
(TALKS/PIANO)
(From Aug-26)

LAV'Y

UP

DN

SAVOY HILL MANSIONS
1st Floor
(June-26/Jan-27)

74

70 71

67 67A

STAIR

LAV'Y

69A   69   68

UPPER PART OF STUDIO
NO. 7 (MUSIC)(Jan-27 on)

66

ROOM ALLOCATION AT DECEMBER 1926

66   ENGINEERING RESEARCH
67:67A   PROGRAMMES:BOOKING
68   OCCUPIED BUT USE NOT KNOWN
69   ENGINEERING ADMINISTRATION
69A   MUSIC CONTRACTS?
70:71   PREMISES/FIXED EQUIPMENT
74   S.B. LINES

BBC
Nameplate/
Electric Sign

UP

VIBULE

HALL

UP

LIFT

WAITING
AREA

AREA

SAVOY HILL

IEE Ground Floor
West Entrance
(February-27) (F2)

IEE CORRIDOR

LAV'Y

UP

DN

UP LIFT DN

ECHO
ROOM

Glass
Doors

LAVATORY

S.B. LINES

STUDIO NO. 8 (DRAMA)

Silence Room/
Observation Window

GREEN
ROOM?

NORTH WEST BUILDING
2nd Floor
(May-28) (H2)

INDEX